CHRIST THE GOLDEN-BLOSSOM

A Treasury of Anglo-Saxon Prayer

CHRIST THE GOLDEN-BLOSSOM

A Treasury of Anglo-Saxon Prayer

DOUGLAS DALES

PAULIST PRESS
New York/Mahwah, New Jersey

Published in Great Britain in 2001 by
The Canterbury Press
9–17 St Albans Place
London N1 0NX

ISBN 0–8091–0542–X

Published in North America in 2001 by
Paulist Press
997 Macarthur Boulevard
Mahwah, New Jersey 07430

www.paulistpress.com

Printed in Singapore

For Sister Benedicta Ward, SLG
With affection and gratitude

'Lex orandi, lex credendi'

CONTENTS

*Principal festivals are in bold type

INTRODUCTION

How did English-speaking Christians pray a thousand years ago? This book is an anthology of Anglo-Saxon prayer and spiritual writing, much of which has never been translated before. Its aim is to make accessible and usable a rich treasury of Christian theology, which was developed in England over a period of four hundred years.

Most of the material in this book was written in Latin, much of it by English Christians; a smaller part was written in Old English. The principle behind this selection has been to set the spiritual writing, of various kinds, within the framework of prayers which were used at the time. There are collections of prayers and readings for the principal Christian feasts and seasons, and also to accompany each of the commemorations of individual Anglo-Saxon saints in the new Anglican calendar.

This material is suitable for private use, and some of it could be used liturgically as well. It has been translated anew throughout to ensure a simple and accessible style, and inevitably there are elements of paraphrase and abridgement. But anyone working with this material is indebted to the scholarly translations which are now widely available, some of which are listed among the further reading at the end of the book. Written before the splits and divisions which have so marred the Church's history, this body of Christian thought and prayer is the common heritage of all English-speaking Christians, and should serve as a meeting ground for Anglicans, Catholics, Orthodox and Protestants. The quest to connect with our spiritual roots and to recover our unity with Christians of other traditions is significant, and this book is intended to facilitate that quest. At the end there is a list of places to visit, where remains of the Anglo-Saxon Church and its culture may still be seen.

History

Anglo-Saxon history often seems remote and obscure; but in fact it is relatively well-documented, and our understanding of it is being enriched all the time by archaeological discoveries. Over four hundred and fifty years of history lie between the coming of St Augustine from Rome to Canterbury in 597, and the Norman Conquest in 1066, during which time the Anglo-Saxon Church and society had to endure the dangerous threat of repeated Viking invasions.

The first period of Anglo-Saxon history, however, lies earlier than 597. By then their conquest of lowland England was virtually complete, but before that time there was a century and half of bitter fighting with the British inhabitants, after the Romans left in 410. By 500, the country was partitioned along its central axis, and many British fled westwards and overseas, the victims of ethnic cleansing. The British were Christian; their conquerors were pagan, and there was deep bitterness.

The second period was an age of Christian mission, as Bede describes in his *Ecclesiastical History of the English People*, when missionaries came from Rome and France, and from Iona and Ireland. This is the time of Augustine, Aidan, Cuthbert, and Bede himself. Even as Bede was writing, English missionaries were active in taking the gospel to the Low Countries and

Germany, with the support of the papacy. Willibrord, Boniface, and later Alcuin all left their mark on European history and its Christian culture.

The third period is dominated by the Viking invasions, which started with a raid on Lindisfarne in 793, and which ended for a time by the mid tenth century when the kings of Wessex asserted their rule over all England south of the Humber. The Church felt the pressure of these raids, and the instability and hardship they brought. Many monasteries were destroyed, while the kingdoms of Northumbria and East Anglia were devastated. The turning-point came in 878 when Alfred the Great defeated a Viking army at the battle of Edington, and was able to impose a truce on his own terms. He and his successors gradually rolled back the Viking advance.

The tenth century is the last great era of Anglo-Saxon history, during which the foundations of medieval England were laid. Backed by secure defences and a steady flow of wealth from minerals and trade, towns flourished and monasteries were created. Dunstan, Ethelwold and Oswald are the dominant figures in both Church and State. During this time, missionary activity was renewed in the direction of Scandinavia.

In the early eleventh century, the Anglo-Saxon dynasty faced renewed Viking invasions, and soon England was ruled by Danish kings including Cnut. But they accepted and profited from the political and ecclesiastical organisation of the land. So too did the Normans, when in 1066 they took over the kingdom and brought the Anglo-Saxon period to its close. Contrary to popular impression, Norman rule did not obliterate the English language and artistic culture.

At the end of this introduction there is 'An Anglo-Saxon Who's Who' to guide the reader in placing the people mentioned in this book, and some of the principal events.

Sources

The core of this anthology is provided by three remarkable prayer books. The first is the *Nunnaminster Codex* (*NNM*), which was probably drawn up sometime early in the ninth century, but which found its way to the royal nunnery at Winchester by the early tenth century. It is full of private prayers, which are mainly meditations on the life of Christ, often addressed to him in terms of respectful intimacy. They are both deep and homely.

The second main source is the *Canterbury Benedictional* (*CB*), which was the official liturgical book of the Archbishops of Canterbury when they pronounced solemn blessings at high festivals in the cathedral. It is rich in its theology and imagery, and reveals clearly how Christians at that time commemorated the Christian year, and venerated their saints.

The third book is called the *Portiforium of St Wulfstan* (*PW*). This was the prayer book of Wulfstan, the last great Anglo-Saxon bishop, who survived the Norman Conquest and died in 1095. He was a Benedictine monk of real sanctity, and these prayers reflect the profound impact made by monastic spirituality upon the English Church throughout its Anglo-Saxon period of development.

The readings are drawn from a variety of types of material, as also are some of the prayers. Homilies, or books of prepared sermons, provided readings intended for liturgical use. Those written by St Gregory the Great are included, because of his profound and abiding influence on the spiritual ethos of the Anglo-Saxon Church and its mission. Bede saw himself as a disciple of Gregory, and his homilies proved of lasting value, at home and abroad, throughout the Middle Ages. In the tenth century, his example was followed by Aelfric, a monk and scholar of Winchester, who wrote many of his homilies in English for use by the clergy of both monasteries and parishes.

The lives of saints, or hagiography, are an important source for the history and theology of the period. They follow a certain pattern established by the classic lives of Antony, Martin and Benedict. In the seventh century, the first life of St Gregory the Great was written at Whitby. Bede did much to help promote the cult of St Cuthbert, and his *Ecclesiastical History of the English People* (*History*) is full of saints' lives. In the tenth century, the tradition was revived to commemorate Dunstan, Oswald, and others. A saint's life in this mould tried to show how the pattern of Christ in the Gospels was replicated in the experience and ministry of a saint, during life and after death.

Personal letters from people such as Boniface and Alcuin are another important and attractive source; so too is poetry. Many of the leading Christians were gifted poets, writing in Old English or Latin, or in both languages; for example, Caedmon, Aldhelm, Bede, Boniface, and Dunstan. Ethelwulf's *De Abbatibus* is a beautiful Latin poem about the spiritual life in a Northumbrian monastery in the seventh century.

There are important works of theology as well, notably Bede's *De Templo*, which examines the spiritual nature of the Church through the description of Solomon's Temple in the Old Testament. Another highly influential writing was Aldhelm's *De Virginitate*, which helped to justify and guide monastic spirituality throughout this period.

Finally there are two important texts from the tenth-century reform of Church and State: the *Coronation Order* that Dunstan drew up, using traditional material, in 973, and the *Regularis Concordia*, formulated at Winchester in 970 by Dunstan and Ethelwold, which governed how the newly reformed Benedictine monasteries were to conduct themselves.

Theology

There is in Bede's *History* a revealing insight into the way Christianity was able to appeal to the pagan Anglo-Saxons and their kings. Edwin, King of Northumbria, took a long time deliberating over whether to accept the new faith of his wife and her Roman bishop, Paulinus. In the end it was his own high priest who declared that, 'if the gods had any real power they would surely have helped me more readily than they have, for I have devoted my whole life to their service'. To this one of the leading nobility added the famous picture of human life as an interlude spent within the relative shelter of a wooden hall during a storm, like a sparrow flying into a building and then out again: 'Human life appears only for a brief while; what comes before or after it? – we have no clue!' These prayers and readings reveal how Christianity was able to respond to this challenge, and to meet the spiritual needs expressed there.

Anglo-Saxon Christians, in their prayers, did not diminish the awesome nature of God as the Ruler and Creator of all things. They were frank about their sense of the smallness of humanity in the face of God. They approached him with deference and care, always fearing lest divine judgement should fall upon any lack of humility. On the other hand, their sense of God was clearly influenced by their human relationships with their own earthly lords. Christ was approached as the truly good Lord, who would respond out of duty and compassion to the needs of his servants. They felt they could rely on that, and this gives many of the prayers an intimacy of address which is memorable and moving.

Their world was hardly secure, nor did most people at that time live a long life. As a result the Anglo-Saxons never became lulled into oblivion about their need of God's protection and help. They also had an acute awareness of the reality of spiritual conflict with evil, which might take many forms. At the heart of their understanding of this stood the cross, to which they showed special devotion in their prayers and in their art. The victory of the cross was mediated to them through the Eucharist, and through the living memory of saints, in whose lives the reality of eternal life might be sensed and seen.

Their perspective of the future was overshadowed by their looming apprehension of God's judgement, a theme also mirrored in some of the works of art which remain. At the same time, this gave them a lively sense of the nearness and reality of heaven. Many of their prayers express a sense of Christian life moving ever onward towards God's kingdom, and again the lives of saints served to intensify this belief. One of the most striking features of the remaining Anglo-Saxon art is the prominence given to angels, and the prayers and extracts from the lives of saints included in this book further enhance this impression.

Central to their perception of heaven and its saints was the Blessed Virgin Mary. Devotion to her is evident throughout the Anglo-Saxon period, and some of the most moving works of contemplative art and prayer express this eloquently. Her example moulded the ethos of monastic life, and coloured also their view of female leadership by abbesses and queens.

Anglo-Saxon Christians venerated their saints in a lively and regular manner, as the material in this book clearly reveals. In addition to the saints of the New Testament, they venerated the saints and martyrs of the Roman Church, and some of the notable missionaries and churchmen of the Church on the Continent too. There were also several royal saints, and monastic leaders, whose lives are now shrouded in obscurity, who have not been included in the second part of this book. But three non-Anglo-Saxon saints have been included because of their special significance for the English Church of this period: Alban, the only known martyr of the Roman period; Benedict, the father of western monasticism, and Martin, the model monastic bishop and missionary.

The style of these prayers is coloured by the richness of their bilingual culture, as they appropriated material common to the western Church at that time, including Ireland, into their own language and spiritual vision. Most of the prayers in this book were written in Latin, but many of them have an affinity with the rhythm and alliteration of Anglo-Saxon poetry in both Old English and Latin. They are permeated also by the imagery of the Bible in a way which mirrors the visual arts. It is a matter of deep regret that not one of their churches now remains with its interior decoration intact, for they were a deeply artistic and creative people.

The Anglo-Saxon Church was created and nurtured to a large extent by monks and nuns, many of whom stood consciously in the Benedictine tradition, as it came to be perceived by the end of this period. St Benedict was commended to the English indirectly by St Gregory the Great, whom they regarded as their own apostle, and who wrote the *Life of St Benedict*. When monastic life was revived in the tenth century, the *Rule of St Benedict* was given a central place in the *Regularis Concordia*.

During four hundred years, the leaders and servants of the English Church proved consciously to be the disciples of St Gregory the Great, whose vision and determination had brought their ancestors the gospel, and whose teaching guided their spiritual vision and the rich culture that gave it expression.

How to use this book

The prayers in this book can be used privately or on retreat; and perhaps on pilgrimage too. Much of the material would lend itself to use in quiet services of meditation, as well as enriching the divine office and celebrations of the Eucharist. In the section called *Temporale*, the prayers have been chosen to weave around the readings for meditation, and to bring out different aspects of the meaning of each part of the Christian year. Many of them will widen our understanding of the liturgy and theology of the season. They are intended also to deepen personal spiritual life, and to enlarge our vision of the Church and of the reality of heaven. Many of them would be suitable as preparation for Holy Communion, and some would be appropriate for use in Holy Week. Most of the readings connect with the saints commemorated in the second part of the book. The intention is that their message and witness should be heard today as part of a clear spiritual tradition lying at the root of our Church's life.

The second part of the book, called *Sanctorale*, commemorates the rich diversity of saints who built up the Anglo-Saxon Church. Some of them, like Cuthbert, Bede and Dunstan, receive special attention because of their pivotal role and the wealth of material remaining. This section draws attention to the significance of people and places, where theology and prayer have been made one. It is intended that as legend and symbolic images are stripped away, the voices of real persons, transformed by the Holy Spirit, can actually be heard. The hope is that we may be inspired by a keen sense of the Communion of the Saints, and especially those of our own land. As they are commemorated throughout the year, we see before us the many-sided work of the Holy Spirit, expressed through each unique individual in various historical and social contexts. Their example should spur on our own mission and discipleship in prayer. Informed commemoration of these saints, at the divine office or the Eucharist, should enable us to sense, as they did, that Christianity comprises a living past sustaining and nurturing our spiritual life in the present and for the future.

AN ANGLO-SAXON TIME LINE

This list gives the dates of death of the saints included in this book. The entries in *italics* mark significant events in the development of the Anglo-Saxon Church.

597   *The Roman mission to Kent arrives in Canterbury*

604   Pope Gregory the Great, who sent Augustine and the other missionaries

605   Augustine, the first archbishop of Canterbury

624   Mellitus, the first bishop of London, and later archbishop of Canterbury

635   *The founding of the monastery on Lindisfarne by Aidan*

642   Oswald, the first Christian king of Northumbria, who invited Aidan

644   Paulinus, the first Roman missionary bishop of York

647   Felix, the first missionary bishop of East Anglia

650   Birinus, the first missionary to Wessex, and bishop of Dorchester-on-Thames

651   Aidan, the missionary from Iona who founded the monastery on Lindisfarne

664   *The synod of Whitby resolves differences between Roman and Irish missions*

664   Cedd, founder of the monastery at Lastingham

672   Chad, the first bishop of Lichfield

676   Ethelburga, abbess of the nunnery at Barking

679   Etheldreda, queen of Northumbria, and founder of the nunnery at Ely

680   Hilda, abbess of Whitby

681   James the Deacon, one of the first Roman missionaries in the north

687   Cuthbert, hermit on the island of Farne, and bishop of Lindisfarne

689   Benedict Biscop, founder of Bede's monastery of Wearmouth-Jarrow

690   Theodore of Tarsus, archbishop of Canterbury

693   Erkenwald, bishop of London

700   Mildred, abbess of Minster-in-Thanet

709   Aldhelm, abbot of Malmesbury and first bishop of Sherborne

709   Wilfrid, abbot of Ripon and bishop of York and Hexham

714   Guthlac, hermit of Crowland

721   John of Beverley, the bishop who ordained Bede

735   The Venerable Bede, monk and scholar

735   Frideswide, hermit of Binsey, near Oxford

739   Willibrord, missionary bishop of Utrecht

754   Boniface, founder of the monastery at Fulda, and missionary bishop of Mainz

782   Lioba, abbess of Bischofsheim

793   *First Viking raid on Lindisfarne marks the beginning of the Viking invasions*

804   Alcuin, scholar of York, and abbot of St Martin's in Tours

862   Swithun, bishop of Winchester

869   Edmund, the martyred king of East Anglia

878   *Battle of Edington, when Alfred the Great first defeated the Vikings*

899   Alfred the Great, king of Wessex

942   *Monastic reform of Glastonbury begins under St Dunstan's leadership*

958   Oda, the first Danish archbishop of Canterbury

970   *The* Regularis Concordia *drawn up at Winchester to govern the monasteries*

984   Ethelwold, founder of Abingdon monastery, and bishop of Winchester

988   Dunstan, abbot of Glastonbury, and archbishop of Canterbury

992   Oswald, bishop of Worcester, and archbishop of York

1012   Alphege, bishop of Winchester, and martyred archbishop of Canterbury

1045   Sigfrid, missionary bishop in Sweden

1066   Edward the Confessor, the last Anglo-Saxon king of England

1066   *The Norman Conquest destroys the Anglo-Saxon dynasty*

1095   Wulfstan, the last Anglo-Saxon bishop of Worcester

TEMPORALE

The Christian Year

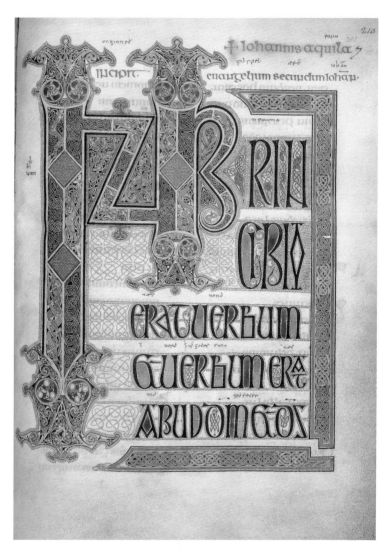

The Lindisfarne Gospels were created early in the eighth century by a group of monastic artists led by Bishop Eadfrith, probably to commemorate St Cuthbert. The intricacy and detail of this opening of St John's Gospel is astonishing, but peeping out of the complexity of its creation is a tiny human face, witnessing the coming of the Word made flesh.

ADVENT

The season of Advent anticipates the final coming of Christ
by reflecting on his coming in history, and also in the hearts
of those who truly believe in him. The sense of
God's judgement exerts an inexorable call upon
a Christian's conscience.

We ask you, O Lord, mercifully to listen to the prayers of your people, that we, who rejoice at the coming in flesh of your only-begotten Son, may attain the reward of eternal life when He comes again in majesty; we ask this through Jesus Christ our Lord. Amen. *(PW)*

O God the righteous Judge, once condemned by men: you have predicted your coming again in majesty to judge the living and the dead. Do not condemn me utterly, O Lord, on that great day. I beg you in all humility that the just deserts of my sins may be mitigated when you come as God in judgement, and that, Lord Jesus Christ, you may set aside all my sins, in accordance with your generous mercy.

Grant that, in union with all your saints who share in blessedness at your right hand, I may be worthy to hear the sound of your voice: 'Come, blessed by my Father, and enter into the kingdom prepared for you since before the foundation of the world', where your saints rest eternally, and all your friends share in your heavenly banquet. Amen.   (*NNM*)

Christ the 'golden-blossom'

My dear people, once again let us consider the noble Advent of our Lord, and how he himself made intercession for us while in this world. Him the patriarchs intimated, the prophets foretold, and the psalmists sang, declaring how he would come from the glorious throne of his heavenly kingdom to possess for himself the kingdoms of men.

All this was fulfilled when the heavens opened and God's supreme power descended upon earth, and the Holy Spirit dwelt within the noble womb, the choice treasury of the Holy Mother for a full nine months. Then the Queen of all virgins gave birth to the true Creator and comforter of all people, the Saviour of the world and helper of souls. The 'Golden-blossom' came into this world, and received a human body from the holy Virgin Mary.

Through this birth we were saved and redeemed, and through this union of God and man we were freed from the grasp of the devil. Through the Advent of Christ we were honoured, enriched and endowed, for Christ lives and reigns with all holy souls forever.

(Blickling Homilies)

Most loving God, you brought forth from the rock a spring of living water for your thirsty people: bring forth from the hardness of our hearts sincere tears of repentance, that we may be able to weep for our sins and obtain by your mercy their forgiveness. Listen graciously to our prayers, and deliver our hearts from all temptation by evil thoughts, that we may become the dwelling-place of your Holy Spirit, through Jesus Christ our Lord. Amen.   *(Regularis Concordia)*

A kingdom open to all

Do not be worried about being a layperson living in the world, anxious that this way of life might prevent you from entering heaven. For the kingdom of heaven is open to everyone, regardless of sex, age or rank, according to the fruit their life bears. Before God, there is no distinction between laity or clergy, rich or poor, young or old, slave or master, but each person will be crowned with eternal glory according to their love faithfully expressed in action.

(Alcuin)

Open, O Lord, the doors of heaven, and visit your people in peace. Send forth your Spirit from on high to enrich our minds, and to attract us to spiritual meditation. Sanctify your people, O Lord, born of a virgin for us, and bless your inheritance with salvation and grace. Give us prosperity in our time, that we may bear fruit while we live here, as bidden by your prophet John the Baptist, who preached in preparation for your first coming. Grant that we may attain to eternal life in your kingdom, with your saints and all your chosen people. We ask this through Jesus Christ our Lord. Amen.   *(CB)*

Grant us your light, O Lord, that the darkness in our hearts being wholly passed away we may come at last to the light, which is Christ. For Christ is the morning star, who when the night of this world has passed, brings to his saints the promised light of life, and opens to them eternal day. Amen.

(Bede – on the Apocalypse)

An artist trained in the Winchester school created this dramatic portrayal of the Nativity, probably in the later part of the tenth century. Its lively use of colour is distinctive. Archbishop Robert of Canterbury, who died in 1052, gave it to the abbey of Jumièges in France.

CHRISTMAS

*Christmas celebrates the coming of Christ into human history
as a tiny baby. Central to the story is the humility of Mary
his mother: her loving obedience made possible the act of
God's self-giving love for the salvation of the human race.*

Eternal and almighty God, the Creator and re-creator of human
nature, by the humanity, which your only-begotten Son
assumed within the womb of the holy Virgin: look with favour
upon us as we welcome the incarnation of your Son. May we be
worthy to be numbered among the members of his body,
through the same Jesus Christ our Lord. Amen.   (PW)

O Redeemer of the world and Ruler of mankind, Lord Jesus
Christ, true Son of God: you are not only powerful but also all-
powerful, the child of a parent but also co-ruler with the
Father, creating all things with him, always by his side, and
nowhere without him. You reign on the highest throne in the
spiritual realm, filling all things, embracing all things, surpassing all things, yet sustaining all things. You can be sensed,
but not seen. You are always present, but can hardly be

found, the one whom no one can justly or unjustly praise.

You deigned to be born of a virgin for the sake of humanity, lost in its sins, in order out of love to rescue our fallen race from the danger of eternal death, and so to restore to it the dignity of your image. For all this I render thanks, and beg you in your loftiness to preserve in me, a wretched sinner, a firm resolve of chastity, purity of mind, and innocence of heart, and all the blessings that you have restored to me; that you may lead me by the grace of a consecrated life to the kingdom of your glory. Amen.   (*NNM*)

Called to the life of an angel

Truly Mary was full of grace, who as first among women, by divine grace, offered to God the most glorious gift of her virginity. By so doing she sought to emulate the life of an angel in response to her experience of seeing and communicating with the Angel Gabriel. Rightly is she acclaimed as 'full of grace' in that she gave birth to Jesus the Christ, the one through whom grace and truth have come in such abundance.

The Lord was indeed with her whom he first raised up to heavenly desires, ardently seeking chastity; and thereby consecrated to himself her human nature with the fullness of his own indwelling divinity. She became a parent while still a virgin, an unique honour, and fitting to her who, as the Virgin Mother, brought forth the Son of God himself.   (Bede – *Homilies*)

I beseech you, merciful Jesus, that as you have graciously permitted me to drink sweetly from your Word which tells of you, to allow me in your goodness to come at last to you, the fountain of Wisdom, that I may stand before your face forever. Amen.   (Bede)

My soul doth magnify the Lord

On this day there descended the heavenly treasure into this world from the throne of our Creator, Jesus Christ the Son of the living God, who came to adorn and honour his bride, that is all who are truly holy. So we must love our Lord with all our lives in response to his generous mercy, whereby he humbled himself to visit us in our exile, to give us healthy minds and heavenly hearts.

We should lead our whole life in meekness after the example of the holy Queen of God, for she perceived that the living Son of God had sought her when she said, 'My soul doth magnify the Lord.' She praised him not only with her words but also with all her heart. She was truly humble who bore the humble and merciful King, who later told his disciples to 'learn of me, for I am merciful and lowly of heart'.

It was fitting too that he should descend to earth through the pure body of a virgin, for he is the origin and teacher of all purity. Christ cannot dwell in the hearts of the unmerciful. Rather we must believe in our Lord, and love him in full obedience: then there will be fulfilled in us his words, 'Blessed are the pure in heart, for they shall see God.' (*Blickling Homilies*)

O author of true blessedness and fount of eternal splendour, who before the world was made was clothed in the glory and honour of your divine nature: you have, however, come to us in such humility, deigning to assume the form of a servant and to be seen wrapped in swaddling-clothes by shepherds. I render thanks to you, and earnestly beg you that whatever I have done out of vanity towards my own body, or in my preoccupation with what I wear, you will forbear and forgive in honour of your own revered clothing while in a human body. Amen. (*NNM*)

May the almighty Lord bless you, and arouse your hearts and minds to heaven, who has consecrated this day to mark the birth of his Son.

May he who is the bread of angels, and who was placed in the manger to be the food of the Church and of all faithful souls, himself enable you to taste in this life the sweetness of spiritual joy, that he may lead you thereby to the fellowship of eternal blessings.

May he, who permitted himself as a baby to be wrapped in mean swaddling-bands, endue you with the finery of heavenly virtues, that you may be worthy to stand before him who is one of the perfect Trinity, to live and glorify him as God forever and ever. Amen.   (*CB*)

EPIPHANY

The word 'epiphany' means the shining of the light of God in the face of Jesus Christ. The feast commemorates the coming of the wise men from the east with their gifts, representing all human races. It also celebrates the baptism of Jesus, and his self-emptying to identify with humanity in its sinfulness.

Almighty and eternal God, the light of the faithful, you have consecrated this feast to mark the first calling of the Gentiles; fill the world with your glory, and subdue all peoples to yourself by the bright light of your appearing. We ask this through Jesus Christ our Lord. Amen.   (PW)

Behold! You the all-powerful Creator of the stars have revealed your incarnation by the witness of a shining star, on account of which the Magi, beholding you, adored your divine majesty with noble gifts. I offer you this sacrifice of praise in gratitude for your Epiphany, and I beg you to be favourable towards me, so that the star of righteousness may always appear in my mind, and in your praise will lie my heart's treasure, O Lord Jesus Christ. Amen.   (NNM)

Christ is the morning star

*Let us consider with care the words of the Gospel, when it says,
'The star came to rest directly over where the young child lay.' This
star was drawn towards the child, not the child to the star. Note
that this star in no way influenced the fate of the baby, which was
born, but this child affected the course of the star by his appearing.
So let no soothsayer or astrologer approach a Christian believer.
Only God the Creator can influence the lives of those whom he created in love in the beginning. Human beings were not made to be
subject to the stars, but stars exist for the benefit and ordering of
human life.*

*The Magi brought their gifts in recognition of him – gold,
incense and myrrh. Gold is appropriate for a king; incense
expresses sacrifice to God; while the bodies of dead human beings
are anointed with myrrh. Therefore these Magi, by their gifts, each
with its own mystical meaning, proclaim him whom they worshipped: a king with the gold, God with incense, and a human
being with myrrh.*   (Gregory the Great – *Homilies*)

Christ our King enthroned on high, whom the ranks of angels
praise sweetly and incessantly: always have mercy.

Christ whom the one Church throughout the world praises,
whom sun, moon and stars, earth and sea serve: always have
mercy.

O King of kings, our blessed Redeemer, offspring beloved of
holy Mary, by the power of your most precious death: always
have mercy.   (Dunstan)

The remarkable Franks casket was made in England sometime in the eighth or ninth centuries, probably at a monastery in Northumbria. It blends Jewish, Christian, Roman and Germanic traditions in a unique manner. In the panel shown here, the coming of the Magi to Christ on the right complements the older Germanic myth of the birth of Weyland the Smith.

Behold the Lamb of God

Herein lies a great wonder of God to be set forth, and we need the explanation of wise teachers to understand this thing. John the Baptist described Christ as 'the Lamb of God', who would bear away the sins of the world. In the former Law, God commanded each household to take an unblemished lamb, and to slay it at Eastertide [i.e. Passover]. They were to daub the sign of the cross with the lamb's blood on their doorposts and lintels. Then they were to roast the lamb and to eat it, and to burn any left over. By this they would be blessed and shielded from the devil.

But this is no longer an obligation upon us. For this slain lamb betokens the slaying of Christ. This cannot be repeated. Indeed this Lamb achieved more when he suffered blows patiently while being offered up for all the sins of the world. He thus suffered as an outcast for us, so that we exiles might return to God's kingdom in heaven.   (Aelfric – *Homilies*)

May God the Son of God, Jesus Christ our Lord, who was anointed by his Father with the oil of gladness above his fellows, pour the blessing of the Holy Spirit on your head by the grace of this sacred anointing, and cause it to penetrate your innermost heart. May you prove worthy to reign with him eternally by virtue of this visible and tangible gift, and so possess each kingdom, temporal and spiritual, on account of your just acts of government. We ask this through Jesus Christ, the King of kings and Lord of lords. Amen.   *(Coronation Order)*

O awesome Majesty, who willed to plunge beneath the floods to liberate from their sins all who are joined to you by baptism. By this sacrament, I humbly pray you to absolve me from my sins, and to bestow on me all your Spirit's blessings, O Lord Jesus Christ. Amen.   *(NNM)*

CANDLEMAS

*The feast of the Presentation of Jesus marks
the fulfilment of God's promise in the Old Testament,
and the first appearing of the Messiah in the Temple.
The traditional English celebration of this feast
with candles is vividly portrayed here in prayers drawn from
the ritual at Canterbury Cathedral.*

May the holy Lord God, the Almighty Father, bless and hallow this fire, which we unworthily sanctify, through the intercession of your only-begotten Son, our Lord Jesus Christ. Today we see him presented in the Temple, being received into the arms of righteous Symeon who had long expected him. You intimated to his prophetic spirit that this child would be the light to lighten all nations and the glory of your people Israel. We ask you, Lord, to bless this light, and all who will take it into their hands. Grant us the true light of your majesty, that we may know you, and by the path of virtue come finally to see you face to face. We ask this through Christ our Lord. Amen.   (*CB*)

imago ui uit

 AGIOS

LUCAS

St Luke tells how the baby Jesus was presented by his parents in the Temple, and here is Eadfrith's portrayal of this evangelist in the Lindisfarne Gospels. The Mediterranean influence is evident in the style of dress, and in the clear lines and sense of light. The saint's title is in Greek, whereas his symbol from the Apocalypse is in Latin.

Lord Jesus Christ, Creator of heaven and earth, King of kings and Lord of lords, hear the prayers of your unworthy servants. May your all-powerful divinity purify our hearts and minds. You created all things from nothing, and ordered that the work of bees should bring this liquid wax to perfection.

Today you fulfilled the prayer of righteous Symeon: we in turn humbly beg you, O Lord, that these candles prepared for the use of all living souls, by land or sea, may be blessed by the invocation of your most holy name, by the intercession of the Blessed Virgin Mary whom we commemorate on this feast today, and by the prayers of all your saints.

Hear the voices of your people from your heavenly dwelling-place as they carry these candles, reverently singing and praising you. Look down from your heavenly throne with favour on all who call upon you, and save those whom you have redeemed with your most precious blood. Amen.   (CB)

God's living flame

Even while he was in his mother's womb, Dunstan shone forth on the Feast of the Presentation of the child Jesus in the Temple. As his mother and all the other Christian people stood in the church at Glastonbury with candles and lamps twinkling, as was the custom on that day, behold! – everyone's light was extinguished by a sudden gust of wind by divine command. While everyone was astonished at this turn of events, miracle was added to miracle.

For the Lord revealed what this meant by giving this sign: He singled out Dunstan's mother with a hidden flame, by which the candle, which she held in her hand, became the first suddenly to burst into light. And so it was that the whole of that holy congregation replenished their lights from the splendour of her light. In this

*way God prefigured that the son that should be born of her, while
still in the womb, was chosen by him to be a minister of his eternal
light.*   (*Second Life of Dunstan*)

O God, the maker and re-maker of human nature, the Creator
    uncreated:
You spread the heavens and founded the earth; you planted
    Paradise and formed humanity from the dust.
You recalled man from error to the way of life, and you gave him
    the Law, speaking from the midst of fire.
You blessed the patriarchs, and called the prophets, for you are
    truthful and without deceit.
You are one and omnipotent, the fount of immortality; and you
    live forever with your Son, our Lord Jesus Christ, and with the
    Holy Spirit unto the ages of ages. Amen.   (*NNM*)

A royal priesthood

*In the Bible, the name 'priest' signifies not just the ordained minis-
ters of the altar, like bishops or priests, but all who shine forth
because of the spiritual stature of their good lives and life-giving
teaching, whose lives are of benefit to many others as well as to
themselves. As they offer their bodies 'as a living sacrifice, which is
holy and pleasing to God', they truly share in the priestly ministry
in a spiritual way. Remember that St Peter did not address these
words only to bishops and priests but to all in the Church of God,
when he said: 'You are a chosen generation, a royal priesthood, a
holy nation, a people chosen by God for his own possession.'*

                                  (Bede – *De Templo*)

Almighty God, keep by your protection the chastity of our
minds and bodies, that under the patronage of Blessed Mary we

may come at last to the wedding feast of your only begotten Son, with our lamps burning brightly, as we run to greet him, saying: 'Hail, holy Virgin and God-bearer, full of grace: from you has arisen the Sun of righteousness to shine upon those who sit in darkness. The righteous old man, Symeon, received him into his arms in joy as the deliverer of our souls, the one who will give us resurrection, even your Son, Jesus Christ our Lord.' Amen.

(CB)

Lord Jesus Christ, you appeared among men in the substance of our flesh, being presented by your parents in the Temple. The old man, Symeon, illuminated by the Holy Spirit, recognised, received and blessed you. Be merciful to us, and endow us with the same grace of illumination by your Holy Spirit; that taught by him we may come truly to know you, and faithfully to love you, our Saviour and our Lord. Amen.   *(CB)*

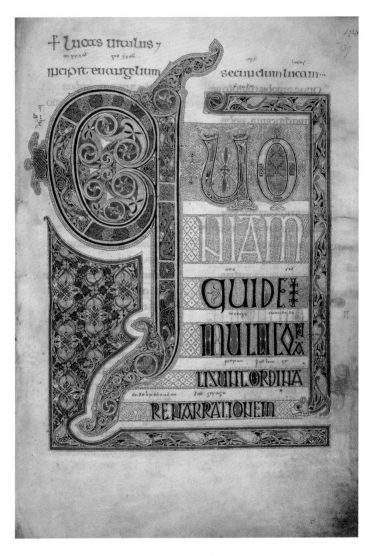

The Irish influence is evident in Eadfrith's initial page for the beginning of St Luke's gospel in the Lindisfarne Gospels. Interlaced patterns and birds fill the brilliant form of the opening letter 'Q', which is highlighted by a multitude of tiny red dots. Within the lines can be seen the later English translation of the Latin text.

LENT

Lent is the season for deepening our repentance
in a more costly and sacrificial way, following the example
of Jesus. It is a time of spiritual conflict,
but also a time of growth towards God's kingdom.
His love brings judgement and forgiveness
as we take to heart the humanity and compassion of Jesus
in his earthly ministry, and in the life
and example of his saints.

Listen, O Lord, we beseech you, to our prayers, and forgive the sins of those who confess to you: that we who stand accused by our conscience may be absolved by your pardon and mercy. We ask this through Jesus Christ our Lord. Amen. (*CB*)

O unique Incarnation of mercy, how can I worthily thank you for the forty days and nights that you, the innocent one, willed to endure for us. You cast down the ancient enemy there in the desert. By this rightful condemnation of the evil one, O my God, protect the weakness of my virtues by your grace, and strengthen them to conquer all my visible and invisible enemies. Cleanse by your utter holiness whatever I have left undone through lust or incontinence, and forgive in your mercy all my past sins. Preserve and protect me now and in the future, and fill me with all virtues by banishing my vices. Remove from my innermost being whatever is contaminated by my sins, for the sake of your profound compassion, and fill me always with the splendour of your divine power, O Lord Jesus Christ. Amen.

(*NNM*)

The servant of the servants

In the morning, Bishop Oswald got up and, as a good athlete of Christ, completed his private prayers, followed by the divine office with the psalms for the day. Then he began to prostrate himself on the ground, heedless of the snow-white hairs on his head or the infirmity of his great age. His sure faith in the Holy Trinity and in its undivided unity sustained and comforted him.

Then this noble bishop began soberly and carefully to wash the feet of the poor, wiping them with a linen cloth and also with his hair, recalling the words of Christ: 'If anyone would serve me, let him follow me; for where I am, there also shall my servant be.' Then he took water in his hands and sang as before some psalms, from the words: 'when I was in trouble I called upon the Lord' to 'who made heaven and earth' [i.e. Psalms 120–134].

When Oswald had finished all fifteen psalms of ascent his brethren bent their knees and worshipped with devotion, saying the final words: 'May the Lord who made heaven and earth bless you out of Zion.' Then holy Oswald also bent his knee with them at the feet of the Lord, and recited the 'Gloria'. At that very moment, as if by a secret sign from the Lord, his holy spirit left his body, and was lifted up to the heights of the heavenly kingdom on 28 February 992. As the poet says:

The courts of God received Oswald on the day before
   March began;
By his prayer he attained to the highest Ruler of heaven.

(First Life of Oswald)

The saint triumphs, the self-offering complete despite the rage
   of evil that pulled down human nature in the beginning.
Wedded to the Lamb and venerated on earth, many are the
   wedding gifts set amidst blazing light.
Your Bridegroom comes, overflowing with grace, to call you to
   harp eternally his new songs.
Now you are inseparable from him, from whom you never
   parted in your earthly life.   (Bede – *of Etheldreda*)

The ladder of penitence

*Let us be mindful now of our daily sins, and all our acts, which are
contrary to God's loving will. Let us with all our power atone for
them with fasts and prayers, with acts of charity and with true
penitence. True penitence means sincere confession of all sins and
an earnest attempt to make amendment for them. Let us weep
now, and remember the Lord's words: 'Blessed are they that weep
now, for they shall afterwards be comforted.' These assure us that
we may with true penitence merit eternal bliss.*

   *Let us be mindful of God's commandments and of our soul's need
while we can. Let us earnestly beseech the Lord to deliver us from
eternal death, and to bring us to the joy of his glory, where there is
eternal bliss in his everlasting kingdom.*   (*Blickling Homilies*)

Almighty and eternal God, spare those who seek to propitiate
you in fear and trembling, and send your holy angel from

heaven to bless and hallow these ashes. May they be a health-giving remedy for all who humbly call upon your name, prompted by conscience on account of their sins. By the invocation of your most holy name, grant that whoever has these ashes sprinkled over them to mark their observance of this holy warfare, may receive health in body and soul. We ask this through Jesus Christ our Lord. Amen.   (*PW*)

Remember, O Lord, the weakness of our human nature, for we justly deserve to be punished as sinners. By the intercession of the blessed and glorious, ever Virgin Mary, and all your saints, spare us in your mercy for we are afflicted sinners. May we who deserve to be scourged for our offences, be redeemed by your holy mercy, and so be healed now and for all eternity. We ask this through Jesus Christ our Lord. Amen.   (*CB*)

PASSIONTIDE

During Passiontide, Christians reflect on the meaning of the suffering of Jesus. Different details of the closing parts of the Gospel story provide food for thought and meditation, culminating in the celebration of Palm Sunday and Holy Week.

O Fountain of all innocence, who wept in public out of compassion for the city of Jerusalem because of the future suffering of its inhabitants as a result of their sins: I thank you, and beg you to give me, a wretched sinner, a fount of tears that I may bewail the enormity of the punishment that befits my sins, O Lord Jesus Christ. Amen. *(NNM)*

Almighty and eternal God, who in the days of the great flood showed to Noah and his family that peace would return to the earth, by a dove bearing an olive branch in its mouth: we pray you that, by the intercession of your holy confessor and bishop, St Martin, these palm branches and sprigs from trees may be sanctified in your truth, which we now offer before you to your glory. May your devout people receive grace and blessing from you as they carry them in their hands, and may they prove

NE EXAVDI
ORATIONEM MEAM·
ETCLAMOR MEVS
ADTE VENIAT ⁘

This decorated initial marks the beginning of Psalm 102 – a lament by God's suffering servant. It is part of a Psalter, produced at Canterbury between 1012 and 1023. David is portrayed as the forerunner of Christ, slaying Goliath, the embodiment of evil. In fulfilment of God's prophecy in Genesis 3, the Christ-like David is pierced in the heel.

worthy to enter with joy into the bliss of Paradise, bearing the palms of victory. We ask this through Jesus Christ our Lord. Amen.   (CB)

Perfection in imperfection

St Gregory taught that 'miracles are the greater, the more spiritual they are: if they are spiritual they are so much the surer.' We therefore consider that the foremost sign of Gregory's sanctity was that he actually followed the example of him who is the beginning of all things.

He resisted being made pope, but in the end relented, despite his own sense of unworthiness. In this Gregory followed the example of Christ, who stooped to become both priest and sacrifice for us. He humbled himself unto death on the cross out of obedience to his Father. He fled all attempts to make him a king, but in the end was offered up by his Father for the salvation of the world, thereby taking the highest place in the kingdom of heaven. But as he did so, he prayed in all humility: 'Father if it be possible, let this cup pass from me.'

Christ followed his Father's perfect will in assuming bodily form, and fulfilled his priestly office when he became obedient to the cross for us. So we too bear our cross after his example. For he who first shunned the kingdom of the whole world gained in the end an empire when he was crucified. Humble and meek, he offered himself for all, even praying for his enemies.

A person who follows in this way, even if the waves of death flow over him, will be very great in the kingdom of heaven. For St Gregory taught us by his own practice as well as by his teaching that 'he asks nothing for his enemy who does not pray for him out of love'.   (First Life of Gregory)

O Almighty God, ever to be cherished and adored, before whom every knee shall bow in heaven, earth and hell: you yourself, as our merciful and compassionate Lord, chose to remain fixed to the ground, bent in prayer, and hemmed in on all sides, out of obedience to your Father's will and authority, beseeching him by whom you were begotten. I thank you, and beg you to show mercy towards my laziness on account of the life-giving drops of your holy sweat. Whenever I am overcome by sleep, and my body is lulled by sloth to interrupt my prayers, do you discount these moments, not for my merits but out of your mercy, by which you battered the ears of your Father in heaven as you prayed on that fateful night, O Lord Jesus Christ. Amen.

(*NNM*)

A martyr-king

The Viking lord, Hingwar, sent messengers to King Edmund of East Anglia in 870, demanding he surrender his people into captivity in return for his own life. The king replied 'It was never my custom to flee, but I would rather die if I must for my own land and people. I will never turn aside from the worship of almighty God, and that he knows well; nor will I betray my love of him for life or death.' He turned to the messenger: 'Say this to your cruel lord: Edmund the king will never bow in this life to Hingwar, the heathen leader, unless he will first bow in my land in true faith to Jesus Christ.'

When he heard this, Hingwar commanded that his forces should first secure the king alone, who had thus despised him. Edmund met him, standing in his hall without weapons, remembering the example of Christ who had forbidden Peter to fight back with force.

They seized and bound the king, and tied him to a tree. They scourged him with whips, while he called on Christ to help him. Then they shot at him with arrows for their amusement. Finally when Hingwar realised that Edmund would never deny Christ, but continued to call upon him faithfully, he cut off his head. So his soul escaped joyfully to Christ, his beloved Lord.

(Aelfric – *Homily on Edmund*)

O height of humility and fortitude of the weak, by your humility you have raised up our fallen world. You permitted the cruel hands of sinners to raise you on the cross, I offer thanks, and pray that by this you will lead me from all wilfulness. Draw me from earth to heaven: do not forsake your lost sheep, but carry me in your arms, that I may be found within your fold, blessed Lord Jesus Christ. Amen. (*NNM*)

Hear us, O Lord, and as you were placated by the prayers and confession of the tax-collector in the Gospel, so be pleased to receive with kindness this your servant who, constant in tearful confession, now seeks with haste your mercy. May he be restored to the sacraments of your holy altar, and thereby be received in the end into the glory of heaven. We ask this through Jesus Christ our Lord. Amen. (*CB*)

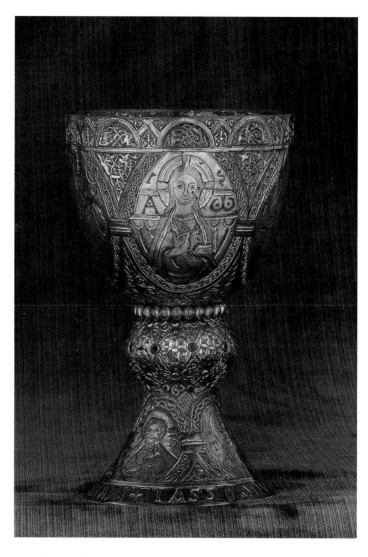

This wonderful silver chalice was given to Kremsmünster abbey in Austria at its foundation in 780, by Tassilo, duke of Bavaria. Its rich craftsmanship reflects English influence and skill, which was highly prized on the Continent. Christ is portrayed here as the Life-giver, the Alpha and Omega.

THE EUCHARIST

The Eucharist was central to the life of
the Anglo-Saxon Church, and churchmen from Bede
to Dunstan commended receiving it regularly.
In art and poetry its meaning was celebrated and unfolded,
and the devotional prayers which remain, are both intimate
and profound.

O God, to whom every heart is open, each desire speaks, and
from whom no secret lies hidden: cleanse by the outpouring of
your Holy Spirit the thoughts of our hearts, that we may desire
to love you perfectly and to praise you worthily. We ask this
through Jesus Christ our Lord. Amen.   (*Regularis Concordia*)

O God, the hope of the poor and the salvation of the humble
and wretched, who having abolished the dark shadows of fleshly
victims, dedicated yourself for us as a living and spiritual sacrifice acceptable to the Father. When dining with your disciples,
you said these words over the blessing of the bread and the
offering of the chalice: 'Take and eat, this is my body,' and again,
'This is the chalice of my blood of the new covenant, which will
be shed for you and for many for the remission of sins.' I thank

you and humbly ask of your mercy that I may be worthy to be redeemed, and made pure and holy by this most holy and life-giving treasure, now and in the future, O Lord Jesus Christ. Amen. (*NNM*)

Streams of living water

When Dunstan fulfilled to Christ the Lord the hours of divine service, and particularly the celebration of the Eucharist, he intoned them with such sincere devotion of heart and mind that he seemed to talk with the Lord himself face to face, as if not at all irritated by the upheavals and quarrels of the people with whom he had been dealing beforehand. Like blessed Martin of Tours, he used always to lift up his eyes and hands to heaven, his spirit never relaxing from prayer. Whenever he was engaged in any other work of spiritual dignity, either at ordinations to the priesthood or consecration of churches or altars, he always shed copious tears, which the Holy Spirit, who ever dwelt within him, drew forth mightily in streams from his eyes. (*First Life of Dunstan*)

Lord Jesus Christ, the way, the truth, and the life: we seek eternal life that you may make us your friends. You came from heaven to pour life into the world; we know you to be the bread of life, the loving bond of human hearts. One who comes to you will never suffer hunger, one who believes in you will never thirst; for you are the true bread, your flesh is all-powerful, and your blood, Jesus, is the true drink of the faithful. By this mystery you redeem us from death, so that we may live in you, Lord, more securely and wisely. We therefore pray you to make us worthy to share in this holy mystery to the praise of your name.

You, Christ, are our teacher to whom we draw near in love; may we be filled with your grace and assistance by this sacrament. May your love be the foundation of our minds and hearts, that we may be kindled with brotherly affection. Grant us peace of soul and mind always, for you are our true peace: preserve us in it, O God. When there is peace, you yourself draw near; where you are may your own be also. Come to us, O Lord, and possess us with joy, that we may become a temple for your Holy Spirit. Amen.   (*NNM*)

Our daily bread

Bear in mind that in the Lord's Prayer we ask for daily not for yearly bread. It is often as easy for a Christian never to receive the food of eternal life, which is the body and the blood of Christ himself, as to receive it just once a year. We should live so that we are truly worthy to receive the Eucharist daily: for someone who is not worthy to receive daily will hardly be fit to receive it yearly.

(*Regularis Concordia*)

I confess and praise with a ready mind your almighty power, O Lord, to whom the angelic powers are subject as they wait upon you. You stooped to serve mankind, and with your most pure hands, by which you made so many wonderful things, washed the feet of your disciples. I render thanks to you, O Lord my God, and by this action of yours I beg you, the most high God, to wash me from my wickedness, and to cleanse me from all that taints my human life, O Lord Jesus Christ. Amen.   (*NNM*)

O splendour of eternal Light, Almighty God, in this feast you gave the precious mystery of your holy body and blood in a secret and intimate manner to your disciples for the salvation of the whole world. You also stooped to wash their feet with your own sacred hands, setting before all people an example of humility, saying: 'If I your lord and master have washed your feet, so you should also wash one another's feet.' We beg you to grant to us your servants on this most holy night, that as we wash externally the feet of our neighbour in observance of the new commandment of your majesty, our minds and all our powers may be thoroughly purged.

According to your generosity, who are the fountain of all mercy, may we be forever cleansed within from all the pollution of our sins. At your leading alone may we merit to attain with fitting jubilation to your eternal banquet, and dance forever before your eternal bride, O God, with palms of victory and with lamps burning bright. May we be worthy to enter in happiness before you, who with God the Father and the Holy Spirit lives and reigns as God in glory for endless ages. Amen.   (*NNM*)

THE CROSS

The cross was one of the dominant motifs in Anglo-Saxon art and architecture. The death of Jesus was regarded as the heroic victory of a self-sacrificing lord, the subject of profound contemplation and meditation.

O thou whose supreme devotion did not refuse the burden of bearing crucifixion, by whom the sins of the human race were taken away as so heavy a burden, when you were uplifted by your own arms like a pure lamb to sacrifice: I beg you to extend the hand of your mercy towards my sins, and to erase all my crimes completely, O noble and resolute Lord Jesus Christ. Amen. (*NNM*)

May you who join all Christian people in venerating this day the memory of the holy cross, and bearing its sign on your foreheads and hearts to protect you from all scandal, be able to enter triumphantly into your share in the heavenly kingdom, with the Blessed Virgin Mary, the holy Mother of God. We ask this through Jesus Christ our Lord. Amen. (*CB*)

The dream of the rood

I seemed to see the Tree, suspended in the air and bathed in light;
It was clad in gold and shining gems, with five stones cross-wise
at its heart.
Stained and injured it was, but joyous in glory too.
Yet through the gilding, the agony could still be seen,
For it bled from its heart, torn on its right-hand side.
Long I lay there, gazing: then it began to speak:
'I can recall being cut down and hauled off to become
a wayside gibbet.
Soldiers dragged me on their shoulders to a hilltop;
my enemies secured me fast.
Then I saw marching towards me humanity's brave King,
coming to climb me.
I could not bend, nor refuse the will of God,
even though earth itself shook.
Stand firm I did, even though if I had fallen,
I could have felled them all.
So I raised the great King on high, while they drove dark nails
into me.
How they taunted us!
I was wet through with his blood after he released his spirit.
Darkness enshrouded us: all creation lamented,
mourning its King's death:
Christ was on the cross.'

Almighty God, Lord Jesus Christ, you stretched out your pure
hands on the Cross for us, and redeemed us with your holy and
precious blood: enable me so to feel and understand this mystery that I may attain true repentance and unfailing perseverance all the days of my life. Amen.   (*Regularis Concordia*)

This cross was made in England in the early eleventh century, and it is now in the cathedral in Brussels. It was designed to hold a relic of the True Cross, and around its edge are inscribed lines that echo 'the Dream of the Rood'. Bearing symbols of the four evangelists and of the Lamb of God, it demonstrates how Redemption and Judgement are at the heart of the meaning of the crucifixion of Christ.

Vexilla Regis

It is told that as St Augustine and his companions approached the city of Canterbury in 597, they were carrying as usual a holy silver cross, and a painted icon of our great King, the Lord Jesus Christ, singing these words:

'We beg you, O Lord, in your great mercy: turn away your anger and judgement from this city and from your holy Church even though we have sinned against you. – Alleluia!'   (Bede – *History*)

You can see the place today and it is greatly venerated where Oswald the first Christian king of Northumbria, on the eve of battle in 634, set up the sign of the holy Cross, and prayed on his knees for God to send help to his people in their hour of need. It is said that it was a cross hastily knocked together, placed in a hole and held upright by the soldiers until they had fixed it into position by heaping up earth around its base.

The king then called his army to prayer: 'Let us all kneel together and call on the all-powerful, ever-living and true God. May He defend us from this arrogant enemy and their cruelty, for He knows that we are fighting in a righteous cause to protect our very life as a people!' All obeyed him, and at daybreak they fell upon their enemy, gaining the victory which their faith deserved.

(Bede - *History*)

Lord Jesus Christ, most glorious Creator of the world, splendour of your Father's glory and co-eternal with Him and the Holy Spirit. You stooped to take our flesh from a pure virgin, and permitted your glorious hands to be nailed to the cross, that you might cast down the gates of hell and so free humanity from eternal death. Look in mercy upon me, an unhappy wretch, weighed down by my sins and contaminated by the taint of my many failings. In your mercy do not give me up, but as a loving father forgive my worst sins and guilt. Hear me as I lie before your adorable and glorious cross, that in the end I may be worthy to stand before you, pure and delightful in your eyes; for you live and reign God forever and ever. Amen.

(*Regularis Concordia*)

In this picture, the women meet the angel at the Empty Tomb, while the guards sleep below. All around them, Spring bursts forth, in the characteristic style of the Winchester school. This Benedictional was made in the last part of the tenth century at Winchester, where each year a drama of the resurrection was enacted in the cathedral, using liturgy and music.

EASTER

**This is the principal feast of the Christian year,
and its accurate calculation was an important issue
in the first century of the Anglo-Saxon Church.
Bede's calculations remain in use today.
Central to the celebration of Easter is the service at night
of the blessing of the new fire.**

O Life of the dying and Salvation of the sick, the only hope of the wretched, and the resurrection of the dead, who rose on the third day, joyful and free, having broken the bonds of death and hell: I beg you with heartfelt gratitude, most high God, to grant unto me in my weakness a part in the first resurrection by the remission of my sins, and a share with your saints in the second resurrection which is without end, O Lord Jesus Christ. Amen.

(*NNM*)

Lord God Almighty, the Light undying and Creator of all light: hear us, your unworthy servants, and bless the light of this new fire, which has been given to us by you, the true Light. May we be kindled by the splendour of your love, and illumined by the fire of true charity. As you transfigured your servant Moses with your wonderful splendour, so deign to illuminate our hearts and minds, expunging the blot of our sins, that we may be worthy to attain to you, who are eternal life; for you live and reign with God the Father and the Holy Spirit forever. Amen. (*PW*)

Day now follows night

From the creation of the world, time was divided so that day was followed by night. On this night of Easter, because of the mystery of the Lord's resurrection, this order of time was changed. He rose from the dead during the night, and on the next day revealed his resurrection to his disciples.

Formerly it was fitting that night should follow day, for by their sin human beings had fallen away from the light of Paradise into the darkness and adversity of this age. But now day follows our night, for it is through faith in the resurrection that we are restored from the darkness of sin and the shadow of death into the light of life by Christ's grace. (Bede – *Homilies*)

O blessed night, which alone merited knowing the time and hour in which Christ rose from the dead. This is the night of which it stands written: 'night shall be as bright as day', and 'the night has become the light of my joy'. The holiness of this night drives away wickedness and washes away sins; it restores innocence to the fallen, and joy to those who mourn. It banishes hostility, and restores peace, curbing arrogance. Therefore in this night of grace accept, O holy Father, this evening sacrifice of incense, which your holy Church offers you by the hands of its ministers, and in the solemn dedication of this candle, made by bees.

We know already the excellency of this pillar of fire, which for the honour of God the sparkling flame kindles. Even if this fire is divided up, its light is in no way diminished. For it is fed by the melting wax which the mother bee has produced to be the substance of this precious candle. O truly blessed and wonderful bees! You neither violate the male sex, nor destroy your unborn progeny, nor damage the chastity of your offspring. Thus did the holy Virgin Mary conceive: she gave birth as a virgin and remained as a virgin.   ('Exultet' in the *Hyde Liber Vitae*)

God with us

By his many appearances, the Lord wished to show that he is present by his divine nature everywhere in response to the desires of those who seek what is good. So he appeared at the tomb to those who were mourning, and he will be present with us in our sadness at his absence. He came to meet those on their way home from the tomb so that they might proclaim the joy of his resurrection: He will surely also be present with us when we joyfully proclaim what we know to be true to our neighbours.

He revealed himself in the breaking of bread to those who invited him into their home, thinking him to be a stranger: He will also be present with us when we generously give what we can to strangers and poor folk. And he will certainly be with us when in the breaking of bread we share in his body, our living bread, with a pure and simple conscience.   (Bede – *Homilies*)

Almighty and eternal God, the comfort of those who mourn and the support of those weighed down: in an act of unique and memorable mercy after your glorious resurrection, you appeared first to Mary Magdalene at the tomb, and comforted her by calling her by name, so that the guilt of humanity might be removed from whence it came. I thank you, and beg you of your immense goodness to accept my prayer, although I am so unworthy, that I may find comfort and reassurance in the presence of your divine majesty, O Lord Jesus Christ. Amen. (*NNM*)

May God, who chose to illuminate this most holy night by the resurrection of our Redeemer, cleanse your minds from the darkness of sin, and make you resplendent with the fullness of all virtues.

May he, who experienced our death, and defeated the forces of hell by his divine power, receive with his blessing these celebrations which you offer today with a sincere mind.

As you hasten to the joys of heaven, with your good works burning like lamps shining bright, may you rise again with all the joyful company of heaven in the eternal resurrection to unending life; through Jesus Christ our Lord. Amen. (*CB*)

ASCENSION

The Ascension celebrates the divine kingship of Jesus,
and his taking human nature into God.
It affirms the nearness of heaven and the reality of eternal life;
for the Anglo-Saxons this was expressed by a strong belief
in the presence of angels.

O God, who today ascended before the apostles to reveal the wonder of your majesty after your resurrection from the dead, give us the help of your compassion, that as you have promised always to be with us on earth, so may we be worthy to remain with you in heaven, who with the Father and the Holy Spirit lives and reigns God forever. Amen. (PW)

May Almighty God, whose only-begotten Son entered this day the highest heavens, bless you, and permit you to ascend whither he has gone before. May he regard you with favour and be pleased with you, when he appears again in judgement as openly as he was seen by his disciples after his resurrection. May you sense him, whom you believe to be seated with the Father in

This picture of Christ as ruler of the universe comes from the copy of the Bible, the *Codex Amiatinus*, which was made at Monkwearmouth-Jarrow, Bede's monastery. It was taken by abbot Ceolfrith on his pilgrimage to Rome in 716, though he died in France. It is closely modelled on sixth century Italian books, brought to Northumbria, and it is the earliest manuscript of the Latin Vulgate text.

majesty, remaining with you until the end of the age according
to his promise. We ask this through Jesus Christ our Lord.
Amen.   (*CB*)

Called to be angels

Once while still a young person and before he became a monk,
Cuthbert was tending the flocks of his master on the hills near the
river Leader near Melrose with some other shepherds. He was
spending the night in prayer as he used to do, full of purity and
faith, when he saw a vision from the hand of the Lord. With his
spiritual eyes, like the patriarch Jacob at Bethel, Cuthbert saw the
heavens open, and angels ascending and descending. They carried
up to heaven in their hands a holy soul, in the form of a ball of
fiery light.

  He immediately awoke his fellow shepherds, and described to
them this wonderful sight, predicting to them that this must have
been the soul of a holy bishop or some other great spiritual figure.
He was soon proved correct, for a few days later they learnt of the
death of the holy bishop of Lindisfarne, Aidan. It had occurred at
the very same hour of the night in which Cuthbert had seen his
vision, and it was now public knowledge.   (*First Life of Cuthbert*)

O Lord the King of glory, always secure on the pinnacle of
  heaven yet merciful to your people: have mercy upon us.
Thou whom the singing throngs of cherubim praise without
  ceasing: have mercy upon us.
The heavenly bands praise you, and the seraphim respond
  singing: 'have mercy upon us.'
Most glorious, unbegotten One, born of a virgin, Alpha and

Omega, surpassing all virtue: have mercy upon us your people gathered here.

Most limpid glory of the Sun and arbiter of justice, when you judge all peoples strictly, we who stand before you beg you most earnestly to have mercy upon us. Amen.   (Dunstan)

We praise thee, O Lord

I urge everyone to render eloquent praise in abundance to God on high, and with hands outstretched to the stars to give thanks to the Lord. He sends winged birds in response to the prayers of his devout people, which flock into the churches, and then fly back to the stars bearing our prayers with them. They present them to God himself for his consideration. How can I describe everything adequately? For angels from heaven descend, shining with light, to carry blessed souls up to the stars. Resplendent with glory, they praise the Lord, decked with crowns of flowers forever.   (Ethelwulf – *De Abbatibus*)

O only-begotten Son of the beloved Father, who appeared alive in many discussions with your apostles for forty days after your passion; and thereafter caused your holy and sinless body to ascend into heaven before your watching disciples, in the sight of hosts of rejoicing angels, to sit above the stars on the right hand of the Father. Grant me grace in all I do, that I may be able to make the journey to heaven secure from all the enemies that may oppose me, O eternal God. May I merit being with you wherever the eagles gather around the body of the Lord. This I beg of you, Lord Jesus Christ, whom the angels serve as Saviour of the world, my Redeemer, and Ruler of all the ages. Amen.

(*NNM*)

May Almighty God extend to you the right hand of his blessing, and pour upon you the gift of his protection; may he surround you with a wall of happiness and the bulwark of his favour, by the merits and prayers of St Mary, blessed Peter the prince of the apostles, and St Gregory the apostle of the English.

May he command his good angels always and everywhere to precede, accompany and follow you, and by his power to protect you from sin or the sword and from all danger.

May he always enable you to prove victorious over your ene-mies, visible and invisible, and may he pour into your heart a steady love and fear of his holy name.

May he permit you to persevere in the right faith and in all good works, that you may complete your days in peace.

May he lead you with the palm of victory into his eternal king-dom. Amen.   (*Coronation Order*)

This splendid picture comes from a Pontifical created at Winchester at the end of the tenth century. In dramatic form, it portrays the descent of the Holy Spirit from the hand of God. He comes upon them as fire, enkindling their minds and their tongues, and also as wind, which blows through the draperies in the turrets of heaven.

PENTECOST

Pentecost celebrates the gift of the Holy Spirit and
the mission of the Church. The presence and reality
of the Spirit can best be sensed in the life of a saint,
and in the conversion of individuals and communities.
The impact of God's Spirit can also be detected within
the structure, order and beauty of the natural world.

O God, by whose Spirit the whole body of the Church is
increased and governed, preserve in us the grace of sanctifica-
tion for the new life which you have given to your family, that
renewed in mind and body, and maintaining unity in the faith,
we may worthily serve you. We ask this through Jesus Christ our
Lord. Amen.   (PW)

O true Giver of eternal light and life, before whom no one can
rise up against me, nor dare to contradict Jesus Christ, the Son
of the most high God, who promised to give the Holy Spirit and
Paraclete to his apostles. I thank you, O Lord Jesus Christ, and
by this promise I humbly beg you to pour your kindness into

every part of my being, and thus guide, protect and rule me. Assist me by the mother of all grace and virtue, and illumine me by the most pure pearl of your indwelling Spirit, O Ruler of the world and lover of complete chastity. May I be ever devoted to you, for I have been created by your wisdom, and am governed by your providence, O Lord Jesus Christ. Amen.   (*NNM*)

The healing of souls

When we want to understand how miracles are wrought by the Holy Spirit, we perceive them not just in acts of healing or raising the dead, but, as our own St Gregory has taught us, more especially in the healing of souls, for therein lies the image of God. In his Homilies on the Gospels, *St Gregory says: 'Miracles are the greater, the more spiritual they are. If they are spiritual in nature they are more likely to be lasting in their effects.'*

St Gregory also taught us to recognise that patience is greater than any miracle. Its strength lies in the meekness and humility of Christ, and the love that fills his being. The foremost sign that Gregory was indeed a saint lies in the fact that he followed the example of Christ in this regard. Therefore Christ helps us more when by his Spirit he speaks to us through the teaching and example of St Gregory, even than when he made St Peter walk across the waves of the sea.   (*First Life of Gregory*)

Come Holy Spirit, without thine aid
Thy praise will never be displayed:
Do thou the grace of tongues bestow,
To whom the gift of speech we owe.
                              (Byrhtferth)

The seven-fold gifts

Seven are the gifts of the Holy Spirit, as the prophet Isaiah declares, and these seven gifts have only been fully seen in human nature in their unity in Jesus, 'of whose fullness we have each received grace poured upon grace'. For each saint has only received 'a penny-worth', in proportion to their capacity to contain the grace of the Holy Spirit.

Abraham received the spirit of wisdom; Moses was endowed with the spirit of understanding. Joshua was filled with the spirit of counsel, and David with the spirit of courage. The spirit of knowledge was revealed in Solomon, and the spirit of devotion in St Peter. In our own days, the spirit of the fear of the Lord was wonderfully manifest in St Oswald, our most notable archbishop of York.

In the natural world, the number seven starts from unity, that is from one, and extends itself with great symbolic meaning unto the pinnacle of its perfection as a universal number.   (Byrhtferth)

O God, my only Redeemer, full of mercy, you have always enclosed within your heart of love the seven gifts of the Holy Spirit and the eight Beatitudes. For this I thank you, most high God, and humbly beg you to remove from my heart the eight mortal sins, and to purify my body and soul from the contagion of all wrongdoing. For you are peace, and resplendent in all virtues, Lord Jesus Christ. Amen.   (*NNM*)

May God, who this day deigned to illumine the minds of the disciples by the indwelling of his Holy Spirit, the Paraclete, fill you with His blessing, that you may abound in the gifts of the same Spirit.

May that fire, which appeared above the disciples, purge the filth of your sins, so that your hearts may shine by the indwelling of his light.

May he who reunited the different languages of humanity in confession of the one faith, enable you to persevere in your belief, and thus by faith and hope to come to appear before his face. Amen.   (*CB*)

TRINITY

On Trinity Sunday, the Church celebrates the fullness
and richness of God's self-revelation, in Jesus and through
the presence of the Holy Spirit. Christians are called
to love God for his own sake, Father, Son and Holy Spirit.
As they do so, their sense of the beauty and holiness of creation
is deepened. The middle prayer here recalls the influence of
Irish Christianity upon developing this sensibility
in the Anglo-Saxon Church.

Father, Son and Holy Spirit, one Almighty God, one in power, in
majesty, in unity and in trinity, eternal Lord who made us and
liberated us, by your power you will save us in the end. Amen.

(*PW*)

Lord God, the Father Almighty, bless and protect us, your servants subject to your majesty, in union with your Son and by the
power of your Holy Spirit; that secure from all our enemies, we
may forever rejoice in your praise. We ask this through Jesus
Christ our Lord. Amen.

(*PW*)

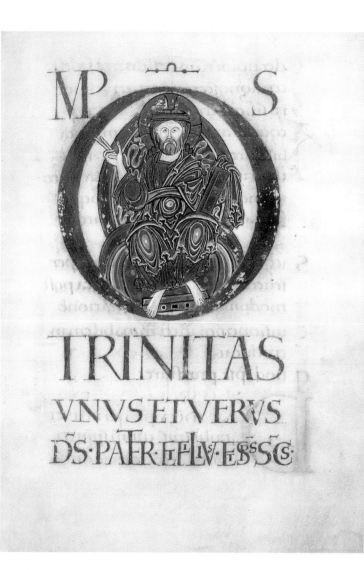

This illuminated initial marks the beginning of a solemn blessing in the name of the Trinity, in the famous *Benedictional of St Ethelwold*, which he commissioned while bishop of Winchester between 963 and 985. The magnificence and artistry of the entire volume mirrors the vision and skill of the monastic reformers of the tenth century.

The mirror of wisdom

The almighty Creator reveals himself by the great work, which he accomplished in the beginning, if only His creatures truly perceived his greatness and so dwelt with Him in eternal glory, being always obedient to him. It is perverse indeed that the thing created should prove disobedient towards its own Creator.

For the world has not always existed; it was God himself who made it, and he exists without beginning in his great glory and majesty, as mighty as he is now, unabating in light and life and truth. It was his original intention to create these wonderful creatures by his wisdom, and to establish them forever in his great love, in the life, which they were to enjoy in all its fullness.

(Aelfric – *on Genesis*)

O Trinity support me, Unity of unity; O Trinity, have mercy
   upon me.
I beg you to assist me, set as I am in the midst of danger, as in a
   great sea.
May neither death, nor the vanity of this world drag me down
   during this year.
I ask for the armies of heaven to defend me with might and
   main,
Lest I be abandoned to the wounds of my enemies.
May the heavenly host go before me to the fortress of heaven,
Cherubim and Seraphim in their thousands,
Led by Michael and Gabriel and all the angels and archangels.
May they defend me in the final intense struggle,
That I may overthrow all my enemies in the end. Amen.

(Lurica of Lodgen: *NNM*)

The service of creation

The creatures of earth and sky obeyed the commands of Guthlac, as did the water and the air, recognising him as a true servant of God himself. If someone faithfully and sincerely serves the Creator of all things, it is hardly surprising if Creation in turn should serve his commands and needs. As Guthlac himself said on one occasion:

'Have you not read how if someone is joined in purity of spirit to God through prayer, everything becomes united to him in God? If a person shuns recognition by other human beings, he will receive recognition instead from wild animals, and will receive visits from angels. For certainly someone who is often interrupted by other people can seldom sense the presence of angels.'

(Felix – *Life of Guthlac*)

Almighty God, you caused your Son to drain the bitter dregs of the chalice of his passion for the redemption of your dying sheep; we who call upon you humbly beg you, the pillar of wisdom, to confirm us in holiness and stability of life, by the sevenfold gifts of your Holy Spirit. We ask this through Jesus Christ our Lord. Amen.   (*PW*)

May Almighty God, the one true Trinity, Father, Son and Holy Spirit, grant you to desire him faithfully, to know him truly, and to love him sincerely.

May he permit you so to persevere in his faith and love, that he may hereafter lead you to the inexhaustible vision of his eternal joy, through Jesus Christ our Lord. Amen.   (*CB*)

SANCTORALE

The Saints of
the Anglo-Saxon Church

Benedict Biscop

12 January

Benedict Biscop died in 689. He founded the monastery at Wearmouth-Jarrow where Bede lived and worked. From his many travels on the Continent he brought back books and works of art to make his monastery a cradle of Christianity in northern England.

Almighty and eternal God, you have made the arduous spiritual journey accessible to your servants by the resplendent example of blessed Benedict your confessor. Grant that we may advance by blameless steps as we follow his example, that we may be worthy to join him with joy in the land of the living. We ask this through Jesus Christ our Lord. Amen.   (*PW*)

A father of monks

Benedict tried to encourage and strengthen his monks, who came frequently to visit him as he lay dying, in their observance of the Rule he had imparted to them. He said: 'Do not think that the rules I have given you were of my own devising. During my life and travels, I visited seventeen monasteries, often on long and dangerous pilgrimages, and I absorbed all I saw and handed it on to you, for your good.'

He also commanded that his vast and magnificent library, which he had transported from Rome and elsewhere, should be preserved as a complete collection and never be scattered or neglected. It was, he insisted, a vital tool for raising the standard of education in our church.   (Bede – *Lives of the Abbots*)

Wulfstan of Worcester

19 January

Wulfstan was the last great Anglo-Saxon bishop who died in 1095. He played a key role in settling the succession of William the Conqueror, and by his own example as a Benedictine monk did much to perpetuate the spiritual traditions of the English Church.

O God, the light of the faithful and shepherd of souls, you sent your servant Wulfstan to serve as a bishop in the Church, to feed your sheep by his word and to guide them by his example. Grant us to keep the faith that he taught, and so to follow in his footsteps. We ask this through Jesus Christ our Lord. Amen.

(Traditional)

'The cat of God!'

Wulfstan avoided all showing off as a bishop, despite the wealth of his see, and carried on wearing the lambskins of a monk. One day, Geoffrey, Bishop of Coutances, teased him in a friendly manner as to why he still wore lambskins when he could be wearing sable, beaver or wolf-skins.

Wulfstan replied that it was quite fitting that Geoffrey and others who had to be wise in this world's affairs should wear the fur of cunning beasts. He in his simplicity would remain content with lambskins. Geoffrey had another go at him, urging him to try on some cat-skin. To which Wulfstan replied: 'Believe me, we sing the "Lamb of God" more often than we sing the "cat of God"!'

(Life of Wulfstan)

Sigfrid of Sweden

15 February

Sigfrid was a monk of Glastonbury who went as a missionary
to Sweden by invitation of the king of Norway.
He became Bishop of Vaxjo where he died in 1045,
having extended his missionary activity
into Denmark.

O God, who sent blessed Sigfrid as bishop to bring the message of
eternal salvation to your servants overseas: grant that as we rejoice
at commemorating his earthly ministry, we may be made worthy
by his prayers to receive the help of your mercy in heaven. We ask
this through Jesus Christ our Lord. Amen.   (*PW*)

The Lord's exile

One who lives alone longs for the mercy of God,
Even if he has to cross the vastness of the sea, sick at heart;
Battling with the oars and the icy weather,
His destiny is to pursue the paths of an exile.

As he wakes he sees only the sea's waves,
The sea birds swimming and preening,
Snow and hail whirl around him, the frost falls.
Then his heart's wound cuts deep, as he mourns for his beloved lord.

Thus he mused as he sat all alone:
Good is the faithful servant;
Care breeds its own cure in the end.
He must go on seeking God's forgiveness and comfort,
For he alone is our soul's refuge and hope.

(from *The Wanderer*)

Oswald of York

28 February

Oswald became Bishop of Worcester in 961 and Archbishop of York in 972. He was a monk and reformer, founding several monasteries, most notably at Ramsey. He was a close friend of Dunstan and Ethelwold. The account of his death in 992 may be found among the readings for Lent.

O God, you adorned blessed Oswald with glory in the greatness of your mercy and gentleness, upon the completion of his apostolic ministry of sowing the seed of the Gospel in the life of your Church. We ask you to favour by his protection the path of your servants that leads to eternal happiness. We ask this through Jesus Christ our Lord. Amen.   *(PW)*

The twin columns of love

Oswald went to Fleury where the relics of St Benedict lay. While there, he stood out as a person founded upon the twin columns of love – of God and of neighbour. This was his sure foundation amidst the storms of this world, for he had true peace in his heart. He embodied the truth expressed by the poet Prudentius:

Peace is the perfection of virtue and the summit of endeavour;
Peace is the reward of battle won, and the recompense for danger.
The stars flourish in peace : earth's lands are bound together by it.
So let a man offer peace above all things, for nothing is sweeter
  to Christ.

Oswald mingled the sweetness of the other life with his sorrows, and so became worthy to receive the gift of contemplative vision in return for his tears, bearing out the truth of the words: 'We cannot rejoice with ourselves and with God at the same time.' He sat in obedience at the feet of God in observance of the holy Rule, desiring with Mary to choose the better part.   (*Life of Oswald*)

Chad of Lichfield
2 March

Chad was an English disciple of Aidan of Lindisfarne, who served as a bishop at York, and later as the first Bishop of Lichfield. In the meantime he lived as Abbot of the monastery at Lastingham. His humility marked him out as a bishop in the Irish tradition, and Bede describes the shrine in the cathedral in which his relics were placed for veneration.

O God, by whose grace the holy bishop Chad became a burning and shining light in your Church. Grant that we may be inflamed with the same spirit of discipline, love and prayer, and ever walk before you as children of light. We ask this through Jesus Christ our Lord. Amen.   (Traditional)

The day of the Lord

He approached the day of his death with joy having always lived in fear and hope for the day of the Lord. For if ever a high wind arose while he was reading or working, he immediately implored God's mercy for the whole human race. Should the storm become fierce, Chad would close his books, prostrate himself on the ground and devote himself to urgent prayer. If it turned to thunder and lightning he would go straight to church and recite prayers and psalms until the weather cleared.

When people asked him why he reacted in this way, he told them that God moves the weather in order to alert people to their spiritual state, and to induce a healthy fear of him. Storms challenge human pride, and remind people of the dreadful day of judgement when God will come to judge the living and the dead, and heaven and earth will be consumed by fire.   (Bede – *History*)

Felix of East Anglia
8 March

Felix came from Burgundy as a missionary to the English, and Archbishop Honorius sent him in 630 to evangelise the East Anglians. He created a school at Dunwich, with teachers drawn from Canterbury. He worked there for seventeen years in close co-operation with King Sigebert, until his death in 647.

May we receive, O Lord, the grace of your blessing by the intercession of your blessed bishop Felix. As we celebrate today his arrival in glory, may we sense the help we request. We ask this through Jesus Christ our Lord. Amen.   (*PW*)

The gift of eternal joy

From the beginning of his reign, King Sigebert promoted the cause of Christianity, greatly assisted by Bishop Felix. The bishop came from Burgundy to Honorius, the Archbishop of Canterbury, to serve as a missionary to the English. So he was sent from Kent to the East Angles.

His hopes were fulfilled, for in due time he reaped a copious harvest of believers. True to his name, he liberated the entire kingdom from evil and pagan belief, and brought it instead to the true faith and the experience of goodness, thus sharing with the people the gift of eternal joy.   (Bede –*History*)

CUTHBERT

20 March

St Cuthbert died in 687, as a hermit on the island of
Inner Farne off the Northumberland coast. For many years
he had been connected to the monastery at Lindisfarne,
founded by St Aidan from Iona, serving as its Abbot and
Bishop. His holy life was celebrated in three lives (two of them
by Bede), and in the creation of the Lindisfarne Gospels.
He remained one of the most influential of Anglo-Saxon
monastic saints, and these prayers are all drawn from the
Regularis Concordia of 970, which regulated the English
monasteries in the later tenth century.

We ask you, O Lord, that the souls of your servants may enter
the fellowship of eternal light, who in this life have followed
after holiness. We ask this through Jesus Christ our Lord. Amen.

O God, you have poured out your gifts of love into the hearts of
your faithful servants by the grace of the Holy Spirit: give them,
we pray, of your mercy, health of body and soul, that they may
love you with all their strength, and by that love do only those
things which are pleasing to you. May they bear themselves with
such humility and discretion in your holy service that their worship may always delight you. We ask this through Jesus Christ
our Lord. Amen.

This lovely cross was found in the tomb of St Cuthbert in
Durham Cathedral in 1827. It was made in Northumbria in the
middle of the seventh century, and was probably worn by the
saint in the closing years of his life as bishop of Lindisfarne.

No hiding place

Cuthbert's spiritual father, Boisil, intimated to him that one day he
would become a bishop. Later in his life, while he was living as a
hermit, Cuthbert refused to tell anyone of this prediction. But
sometimes he hinted at it to brethren who came to visit him,
declaring with much sorrow: 'Even if I could hide myself away on a
tiny island, in a cell surrounded by the waves of the sea, cut off
from all contact with human affairs, even there I know I would not
be immune from the snares of this deceptive age. I would always
dread the possibility that love of wealth and power would somehow
tempt me and lure me away.'   (Bede – *Life of Cuthbert*)

I thank you, holy Lord, almighty Father and eternal God, for your protection this day. Grant me tonight cleanness of heart and chastity of body, so that in the morning I may be able to pay worthy service to you. Hear my prayer and deliver me from all temptations and evil thoughts, that I may become the dwelling-place of your Holy Spirit. I ask this through Jesus Christ our Lord. Amen.

The final conflict

I was anxious to return to Cuthbert on the island of Inner Farne because of his illness, but for five days was prevented from sailing because of a storm. This was however part of God's plan. He wished to test him further by bodily pain, through a still fiercer conflict with his ancient enemy while he was cut off from human company. When we finally reached him, I stayed behind to nurse him, bathing his ulcerated foot in warm water, and offering him some heated wine. I could see from his face that he was worn out by lack of food and by disease. Finally I got him to speak to me.

'For five days and nights I have not stirred from my bed. This was my food during this time.' He showed me five onions concealed beneath his bedding. 'As often as my mouth became parched and burnt through thirst and dryness, I tried to refresh it by tasting one of these.' Yet when I looked, less than half of one of the onions had been nibbled away. 'My enemies have never persecuted me so insistently during all my time on this island as during these last five days.'

When his illness reached its crisis, and he knew that the time of his death was near, we carried him back at his request to his little cell and place of prayer, because it was too painful for him to walk. I entered later that day, and found him lying in the corner of his oratory, opposite the altar. He said very little because of his illness. His final advice to us was: 'Always keep peace and divine

*charity among yourselves, and when you have to make a decision
as a community seek unanimity.'*

*He continued quietly watching and praying throughout the
night. When the time of the night office came, and he had received
Holy Communion from me to assist him on his way, he raised his
eyes to heaven, and lifting up his hands sent forth his spirit in the
very act of praising God, and so passed to the joys of the kingdom
of heaven.*   (Bede – *Life of Cuthbert*)

Lord Jesus Christ, I adore you ascending the cross: may your
   cross free me from all assaults of evil.
Lord Jesus Christ, I adore you wounded on the cross: may your
   wounds heal my soul.
 Lord Jesus Christ, I adore you laid in the grave: may your death
   bring me life.
Lord Jesus Christ, I adore you descending into hell to liberate its
   captives: I beg you never to let me enter there.
Lord Jesus Christ I adore your resurrection and ascension: have
    mercy on me.
 Lord Jesus Christ, I adore your coming in judgement: when you
   come, do not enter into judgement with me, a sinner, but
   come rather to forgive than to condemn me.

May the prayers of the blessed and ever-virgin Mary, the Mother
of God, of St Peter your apostle, of St Benedict your confessor,
and of all your saints, and the sincere intercession of this community make peace with you, O God, for the soul of our brother
who has died. May he obtain forgiveness of all his sins; preserve
him from punishment in the flames of hell, for you have
redeemed him by the glorious blood of your Son, our Lord Jesus
Christ, who lives and reigns with you and the Holy Spirit forever
and ever. Amen.

Guthlac of Crowland
11 April

Guthlac died in 714 having lived for many years as a hermit in the fens at Crowland. His *Life* was written by Felix, who modelled it on Bede's *Life of Cuthbert*. Guthlac regarded St Bartholomew as his patron and protector, and some of his teaching may be found among the readings for the season of Trinity.

Almighty and eternal God, your wonder is always and everywhere proclaimed in the achievements of St Guthlac your monk. We crave your mercy, that as you have borne him away to great glory, so by the aid of his prayers you may ever assist us by your grace going before us. We ask this through Jesus Christ our Lord. Amen.   (PW)

The fen fastness

When Guthlac heard about the place, he took a fisherman's boat and penetrated the fastness of the fen until he came to the island called Crowland. It is a remote and uninhabited place, unfrequented and little known. No one had been able to endure living there before Guthlac, the servant of Christ, because it was believed to be haunted by demons.

Guthlac began to live all alone, with only God to help him, as he showed his contempt for the enemy by pursuing the solitary life in the woods there. The day of his arrival was the feast of St Bartholomew, and he placed his confidence in that apostle's help. He loved its isolation and regarded the place as God's gift to him. So he made a solemn vow to remain there all his days.   (Felix – *Life of Guthlac*)

Alphege the Martyr

19 April

Alphege was Archbishop of Canterbury between 1005 and 1012. Viking raiders seized him as a hostage in Canterbury, and because he refused to offer them any ransom at the expense of his people, he was brutally killed at Greenwich. He was a monk and protégé of Dunstan's, who appointed him Abbot of Bath and, in 984, Bishop of Winchester.

May God, who is the glory of his saints and the victory of his martyrs, guard us by his divine generosity, and by the protection of blessed Archbishop Alphege; that holiness may flower within us and through us in all our service of God. We ask this through Jesus Christ our Lord. Amen.   (*CB*)

A martyr for justice

The new Norman Archbishop of Canterbury, Lanfranc, was uncertain about the sanctity of many of the English saints. He raised the case of Alphege with St Anselm, later his successor as Archbishop of Canterbury. Anselm replied: 'It is clear that someone who would rather die than sin against God even in a small matter would certainly rather die than anger God by falling into serious sin.

'It would appear to be a graver sin to deny Christ than for a lord to injure his men by causing them to be robbed of their wealth. But it was this lesser crime which Alphege refused to consider. So we can be sure that he would never have denied Christ if evil men had forced him to do so. We can therefore see that justice ruled his heart in a wonderful way, since he would rather die than cause a scandal

to others. I therefore consider that someone who has truly preferred death in the cause of justice should, like St John the Baptist, be considered a martyr.' (*Life of Anselm*)

Mellitus of London
24 April

Mellitus was one of the second group of missionaries sent by Pope Gregory the Great in 601. He was an abbot from Rome, whom Augustine made the first Bishop of London. In 619, he became the third Archbishop of Canterbury, dying in 624.

Attend, O Lord, to our prayers, which we offer in commemoration of your holy confessor and bishop Mellitus: for we place no trust in our own righteousness, and seek help from him whose prayers please you. We ask this through Jesus Christ our Lord. Amen. (*PW*)

Enflamed with divine love

Mellitus suffered poor health, but was otherwise active in mind and vigour. His heart was in heaven, and his noble birth was transformed by prayer into true nobility of spirit. He was a person of real spiritual power, as this story will reveal.

Once there was a serious fire in Canterbury, which threatened the residence of the Archbishop. It was proving impossible to extinguish it with water, so Mellitus, full of faith, ordered that he be carried out and placed in the path of the fire. There was a church dedicated to the Four Crowned Martyrs hard at hand, and there the bishop prayed. Immediately, the south wind, which had been fanning the blaze, swung round to the north, and gradually the fire died out of its own accord.

He was a man enflamed with divine love, and so was able to act in protection of his people. (Bede – *History*)

Erkenwald of London
30 April

Erkenwald was appointed to be Bishop of London by
Archbishop Theodore. He was a wealthy and holy person who
founded monasteries at Barking and Chertsey. For a time he
ruled Chertsey as its Abbot, while his sister Ethelburga
presided over Barking. He was able to reconcile Theodore and
Wilfrid before his death in 693.

We seek your mercy, O Lord, at the intercession of your blessed
confessor and bishop Erkenwald. Incline to us in your compassion, and look with favour upon us sinners as a result of his
prayers. We ask this through Jesus Christ our Lord. Amen.

(*PW*)

A holy bishop

*Theodore appointed Erkenwald to be Bishop of London. He is
remembered for his great holiness before and during his episcopate,
so that even to this day the carriage which he used is regarded as
miraculous, and splinters of it are used to cure people.*

*Before he became bishop he founded two monasteries, one for
himself and one for his sister, Ethelburga. He established a high
standard of monastic life within them. His was in Surrey on the
river Thames, at Chertsey, then an island. His sister's community
was at Barking in Essex. She ruled over her sisters as a mother, and
proved no less holy than her brother in her pastoral care of others.*

(Bede – *History*)

John of Beverley

7 May

John was a monk of Hilda's abbey at Whitby, who had also studied at Canterbury under Archbishop Theodore and his companion, Abbot Hadrian. In 687 he became Bishop of Hexham with a lasting reputation for compassion and holiness, and he it was who ordained Bede as deacon and later as priest. He died in 721 in the monastery he had founded at Beverley.

O God, you gladden our hearts each year by this celebration of your blessed bishop John. We beg you that he may serve as our intercessor in heaven, who while he lived on earth preached tirelessly in your name. We ask this through Jesus Christ our Lord. Amen.   (*PW*)

'I wish you a speedy recovery!'

Once while the bishop was visiting an estate to dedicate a new church, he was asked by its lord to visit one of his young servants who was dangerously ill. When the bishop entered the room he found an empty coffin lying ready beside the dying man. He simply said a short prayer, blessed him, and left with his usual comforting words, 'I wish you a speedy recovery!'

Later during the meal, the servant boy sent a message to his master asking for a drink. The lord was delighted, and sent him a cup of wine, which the bishop had duly blessed. The last of the illness departed, and the youngster got up, got dressed, and went in to greet the bishop and join the party.   (Bede – *History*)

This is the only work of art remaining which can be attributed to St Dunstan. It is found in a manuscript that he edited while abbot of Glastonbury. As a powerful line drawing, it might have been a design for a vestment, or metal relief, or for a fresco. It shows the saint at the feet of Christ, the Wisdom of God. His rod symbolises the Kingdom of God, and on the book in his hand are inscribed words from the Bible used by St Benedict at the beginning of his *Rule*.

DUNSTAN

19 May

By the close of the Anglo-Saxon period, Dunstan was
regarded as one of the greatest of English saints.
He lived between 909 and 988, and his active life as
a churchman was divided between being Abbot of Glastonbury
for nearly twenty years, and Archbishop of Canterbury
from 960 until his death. To his leadership of the Church
and the renewal of its monasteries, he brought many
personal gifts as an artist, musician, and craftsman,
mystic and spiritual father.

O eternal God, you enriched blessed Dunstan with many
virtues, and endowed him with grace poured upon grace, so that
as he was always untiring in his love of you on earth, he might
contemplate unceasingly the vision of your blessedness. You
made him faithful in the care of your Church, and now you have
set him over all your good things, filling him with blessing and
joy. We pray that, in your all-powerful mercy, we may be loosed
from the bonds of our sins by his merits, and being confirmed
in our own holy vocation, we may attain to the glory of your
heavenly kingdom, where each person arriving hears your
words: 'Well done! good and faithful servant.' We ask this
through Jesus Christ our Lord. Amen.   (*Memorials of St Dunstan*)

Hail! Dunstan, noble bishop and shining star, true light of the
English people and our leader to God. You are our greatest hope
and treasured sweetness, breathing upon us the fragrance of
balsam and the honey of life. We trust in you, father, even

though we seem no longer to please you. We stretch out our hands to you, and pour out our prayers before you.

Your sheep are being scattered and hard-pressed, beloved shepherd. Behold! We Christians are being killed by the sword of a barbarian people. Offer to Christ for us acceptable prayers and sacrifices, that he may be placated and undo the chains of our sins, because of which an unbelieving people and an evil pestilence have swept over the lands of the English, and the children of your Church.

May the hope of the Father, the peace of the Son, and the light of the Holy Spirit be with us forever as a result of your prayers. Amen.   (*Memorials of St Dunstan*)

The renewal of Glastonbury

At the king's command, Dunstan the servant of God, became Abbot of Glastonbury, and ruling with great grace following the Rule of St Benedict, he shone forth as the foremost abbot of the English church.

As a prudent shepherd he secured in every way the enclosure of the monastery and provided for it. There he gathered the sheep of the Lord from far and wide, lest they be slain by the invisible wolf. As their teacher he fed them with the Word of God, and from the eternal spring within him, nourished them with instruction in the Bible, teaching them how to pass through the painful paths of this life to the eternal delights of the heavenly banquet.

It quickly became clear that in a short time Dunstan had successfully sown Christ in the hearts of his disciples, who had come to him young and unformed in the faith. They flourished under his rule and bore the fruits of good works. So that from then until now,

many pastors of churches were taught by his instruction and exam-
ple, and were sought after to rule in various cities and monasteries
according to the holy Rule and the principles of justice. Indeed, no
one having been his disciple could fail to seek after the highest joys
of heaven, having been exposed to his influence and example.

(*First Life of Dunstan*)

I beg you, merciful Christ, to protect me, lest the storms of the
underworld swallow me up!   (Dunstan)

Alleluia! Come beloved Dunstan, and pray for your humble servants before the throne of Christ in the heavenly kingdom.

(Byrhtferth)

A holy death

From the day of the Lord's ascension, this pillar of God began
slowly to lose his strength; weariness prevailed and Dunstan took to
his bed. For a full six days and nights he was intent on heaven, and
comforted by coming and going in the Lord. On the morning of the
Sabbath, after the divine office of Matins had been completed, he
summoned the holy community of his brethren to see him. He
again commended his spirit to their prayers, and received from the
altar the viaticum of the sacraments of Christ, which had been cel-
ebrated in his presence. Giving thanks to God, he began to sing:
'The merciful and gracious Lord hath so done his marvellous deeds
that they ought to be held in remembrance: he hath given food
unto those who fear him.'

With these words on his lips, he rendered his spirit into his
Maker's hands, and rested in peace. O how happy him whom the
Lord found thus watching! He was buried in a grave of his own

*preparing, in the cathedral at Canterbury where he had taught his
own people, while as a bishop he had passed among them.*

(*Second Life of Dunstan*)

O merciful confessor of Christ, O light and teacher of the
English people: O Dunstan, the good shepherd and upholder of
our whole land! Be the healer of the various ailments of those
who visit your tomb. As we now abase ourselves before your
holy merits, which stand confirmed before heaven's high throne,
pray to God to deliver our land from its enemies, loose us from
the bonds of our sins, and lead us, we pray, to eternal life in the
end. We ask this through Jesus Christ our Lord. Amen.

(*Memorials of St Dunstan*)

May God, the light of all the ages, who caused the noble and
eminent bishop Dunstan to shine forth in our times like one of
the apostles, fill you with heavenly blessing on account of his
merits; that following the footsteps of so resplendent a predecessor, you may be able to mount the ladder of divine ascent.

May he who foreordained that so venerable, glorious, unique
and angelic a patron should arise for all the English people,
kindle in you a burning desire to reach the place where this
magnificent saint ever flourishes among the choirs of the angels
in heaven. Amen.

(*CB*)

Alcuin of York

20 May

Alcuin was educated at York and in 781 became adviser
to Charlemagne. As Abbot of Tours, he was one of
the most influential reformers and intellectuals of
the Frankish Church, presiding over
an important school there. He wrote extensively,
and many of his letters survive. He died in 804.

Eternal Light shine into our hearts; eternal Goodness deliver us
from evil; eternal Power be our support; eternal Wisdom scatter
the darkness of our ignorance; eternal Pity have mercy upon us:
that with all our heart and mind and soul and strength we may
seek your face, and so be brought by your infinite mercy into your
holy presence; through Jesus Christ our Lord. Amen.   (Alcuin)

My dear son

*Though in body you are still a boy, be a man in character, firm and
purposeful, devoted to the work of God. Be prayerful, gracious in
obedience, truly humble and peaceful in your speech, and sincerely
penitent. Be full of love for God and cheerful in hope, trusting in
the goodness of God. Be loving at home, and towards your parents.*

*Learn so that you may be able to teach, knowing that God will
speak through you as you read the Bible, and when you pray to
him sincerely and with compunction. What is sweeter than to
speak with God? Think of him as always present with you, and
that will always protect you from sin, and keep you clear and clean
in his sight.*   (*Letters of Alcuin*)

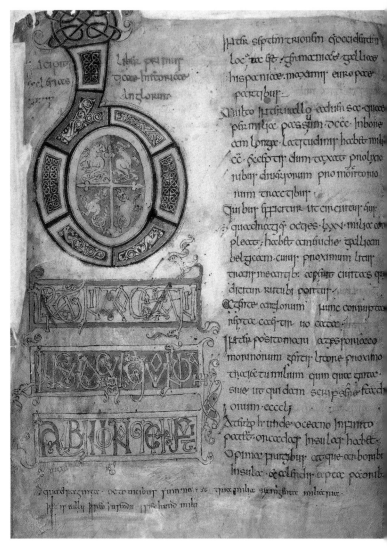

This copy of Bede's *History* was written in the early ninth century, possibly at Canterbury. Its decoration resembles that found on contemporary jewellery. There are English glosses to help interpret the Latin text.

BEDE

25 May

**Bede is the only Englishman to be regarded as a Doctor
of the Church. He spent almost all his life in the monastery of
Wearmouth-Jarrow, where he died in 735. His *History*
gives a full and unique picture of the earliest English Church,
but most of his work was expounding the Bible.
He also compiled saints' lives, notably two for St Cuthbert,
and was interested in science and the calculation of time.**

Oh God, the light of our fathers and the rock of their whole
strength, grant us the diligence of your servant Bede to study the
noble works you accomplished in their days, that we may discern and trust your power in our own; through Jesus Christ our
Lord. Amen.   (Traditional)

O God, you can see that we are set in the midst of such dangers,
that because of the fragility of our human nature we can hardly
remain steady in our life and vocation; give us health of body
and mind, that whatever we have to endure because of our sins,
we may overcome with your help. We ask this through Jesus
Christ our Lord. Amen.   (*NNM*)

The love of learning

*I was born on the lands of this monastery at Jarrow, and when I
was just seven years old I was placed by my family into the care of*

the holy Abbot Benedict Biscop, and later that of Abbot Ceolfrid, for my education. Since then I have passed all my life in this community, studying the Bible, following the monastic Rule, and daily singing the divine office in church.

It has always been my chief delight to learn, or to teach, or to write. At the age of nineteen I was made a deacon, and at the age of thirty I was ordained a priest by Bishop John of Beverley, at the command of my abbot, Ceolfrid. Throughout my priesthood, I have drawn from the commentaries of the fathers on the Bible, adding notes of my own to clarify the meaning and sense of Scripture, for my own benefit and that of my brethren.

(Bede – History)

Facing that journey which no one can escape,
Each must be as careful as he has need to be.
Let him contemplate before he departs from this life,
How things may fall out for his spirit, for good or ill,
After the day of his dying.

(Bede's death-song)

'Good! It is finished'

One of us remained with him while the others went to church, and said to him: 'There remains just one more chapter to be completed in that book which you were dictating. But perhaps it is now hard for you to answer any more questions?' He replied: 'Not at all: take up your pen, sharpen it and proceed with all speed!' This we did.

At three o'clock, he broke off and told me to call together the priests of the community: 'I have some little treasures in my box, pepper, linen cloths and incense: let me share out God's gifts.' He said to them: 'Now the time has come for me to leave my body and return to my Creator, to him who formed me out of nothing. I have had a long life, and he, as a just Judge, has provided for me well all along. My death is near, and my soul longs to see Christ the King in all his beauty.'

As evening drew on, one of the young boys, called Wilberht, asked him again: 'There remains still one sentence that we have not yet completed, beloved Master.' Bede said: 'Write it down now!' 'There!' said the boy, 'that's finished.' To which Bede answered: 'Yes. It is indeed finished: you have spoken truly. Now support my head in your hands, for I want to sit in my holy place where I have always prayed, so that I may call now upon my Father in heaven.'

Then sitting on the floor of his cell and singing the 'Gloria', Bede died. Everyone said that they had never seen someone end his days in such peace and sanctity.   *(The Letter of Cuthbert)*

O God the visitor of the humble, who consoles us by brotherly love, bestow upon our community your grace, that we may sense your coming among us through our guests in whom you dwell. We ask this through Jesus Christ our Lord. Amen.   *(PW)*

Bless, O Lord, this community, which seeks to receive the grace of your benediction. Extend your own hand from heaven to touch the head of each member here. Let the abundance of your blessing fall upon this your family, as the dew descends to water the face of the earth. May your hands bestow the embrace of the Holy Spirit to bring us joy, that your blessed ones may remain secure for all eternity. We ask this through Jesus Christ our Lord. Amen.   *(CB)*

Aldhelm of Malmesbury

25 May

**Aldhelm was as learned a scholar as Bede, although fewer of
his works survive. His most lasting influence was upon
Latin poetry in England. As Abbot of Malmesbury he exercised
a wide political and intellectual influence in Wessex
and elsewhere. He became the first Bishop of Sherborne
in 705, and died in 709.**

We beg you, O Lord, that by the joyful intercession of your
blessed confessor and bishop Aldhelm, we may so benefit by his
holy teaching, that we may be made worthy to celebrate his festi-
val with all joy. We ask this through Jesus Christ our Lord.
Amen.   (PW)

The image and likeness restored

*I have portrayed so far the beauty of virginity freely chosen, and
the attractions of chastity, in all the many colours of their splendour, mirroring those of flowers, or as an artist might adorn portraits of kings and nobles with gilt and chased ornamentation. An
artist may himself be sickly and unattractive as a person, but his
subject is royal and is worthy of decoration and praise, so that it
can be revered rather than the artist himself.*

*I call to mind the words of the Bishop of the Apostolic See, St
Gregory himself, when he proclaimed; 'As an inadequate painter, I
have portrayed a beautiful person; even I, who am still being tossed
about on the waves of my own sinfulness, but who seek to point
others to the safe haven of perfection.'*   (Aldhelm – *On Virginity*)

AUGUSTINE

26 May

St Augustine was sent from Rome to Kent by
Pope Gregory the Great in 597 to bring Christianity to
the Anglo-Saxons. He led a company of monks, drawn from
Gregory's own monastery on the Caelian hill in Rome.
He created the cathedral at Canterbury and was
its first Archbishop, but his mission depended heavily upon
the support of King Ethelbert and Queen Bertha for its
initial success. The partnership between Church and Crown
remained close throughout the Anglo-Saxon period.

O God, who sent the holy bishop Augustine to shine forth as the glory and consecrated herald of the earliest English church; grant we pray, that we who celebrate today his annual feast on earth may become worthy by his patronage to rejoice with him in heaven. We ask this through Jesus Christ our Lord. Amen.

(PW)

O God, you rule your people in love and care for them in virtue, give to this your servant the spirit of wisdom and disciplined rule; that committed to you with all his heart, he may always remain capable to rule in your kingdom. Under your guidance may the security of your Church be upheld in his time, and may the Christian religion flourish in peace. May he so persevere in good works that, by your guidance, he may attain to your heavenly Kingdom. We ask this through Jesus Christ our Lord. Amen.

(Coronation Order)

Christ-like missionaries

As soon as Augustine and his companions reached their new home in Canterbury, they began to imitate the apostolic way of life of the earliest Church. They prayed constantly, with vigils and fasting. They preached to all they could, and despised worldly possessions, accepting only the necessities of life. They always practised what they preached, and were quite prepared to endure adversity and suffering, even martyrdom, for the truth they proclaimed. Their example attracted many to faith and baptism, and they used the ancient church of St Martin as their first base for mission until the king gave them permission to preach more widely.

In the end the king and his family were converted and baptised, convinced by the life of the missionaries, the promises they declared, and the miracles which accompanied their preaching. More and more people became Christians, but the king compelled none to convert, although he tended to favour those who did. But he had learnt from Augustine that the service of Christ was voluntary, and that any compulsion was therefore wrong.

(Bede – *History*)

O God, the immortal defender of all who approach you: you offer liberation to the suppliant, and peace to those who seek you, life to the faithful, resurrection to the dead, hope to the loyal, glory to the humble and blessings to the just. You have commanded the fullness of your precepts in your great love, so that in us who offend in so many things, your love may abound yet more to cleanse us from all sin. Hear our prayer, which we make to you through Jesus Christ, your Son, our Lord. Amen.

(*NNM*)

This lovely crucifix from the late Anglo-Saxon period was designed to hold a relic. Symbols of the four evangelists appear at the extremities of the cross. Bede describes how St Augustine approached the city of Canterbury in 597 carrying a cross made of silver, and an icon of Christ.

'Your prayers are at work where you cannot be'

Pope Gregory writes to Eulogius, Bishop of Alexandria, in 598

I am glad to tell you that I decided, supported by your prayers and prompted by God, to send a monk of my own monastery to preach the gospel to the English people, who, placed in a remote corner of the world, worship only images of stone and wood. With my permission he has been made a bishop by the Frankish bishops, and has reached those people with their assistance.

Letters have now reached us telling of his safety and of the successful work of him and his companions. The miracles of the first apostles seem to be being re-enacted through them. On Christmas Day, more than ten thousand English people were baptised by him, our fellow-bishop and brother.

I am informing you of this development so that you may see more clearly what you achieve, both by your own ministry of preaching in Alexandria, and at the very end of the world by your prayers. For your prayers are at work where you cannot be, while your holy deeds are apparent where you are.

O God, who prepared and establishment of the Roman Empire for the preaching of the gospel of your eternal kingdom, stretch out your heavenly arms over your servant our ruler, that the peace of the churches may not be disturbed by the storms of war. We ask this through Jesus Christ our Lord. Amen.

(Coronation Order)

May God, who through the apostolic preaching of blessed Augustine brought knowledge of himself to the English people, give you absolution from your sins, strengthen you in virtue, and give you true compunction of heart.

May he who now rejoices in heaven for the work he accomplished here on earth for your benefit, always defend you with his paternal care and pray to God for you, that you may come to rejoice with him in eternal blessedness. Amen.   *(CB)*

Oda of Canterbury
2 June

Oda was Archbishop of Canterbury from 942 until his death in 958. He was of Danish descent, and went to the Continent on diplomatic missions while Bishop of Ramsbury. He was professed as a monk at Fleury, where the body of St Benedict lay, and he was the moving force behind the revival of Benedictine monasticism in Wessex, initiated by Dunstan's appointment as Abbot of Glastonbury.

We seek your mercy, O Lord, by the intercession of your blessed Archbishop Oda. Hear us with favour, that as we celebrate this anniversary of his repose, we may be commended to you by his prayers. We ask this through Jesus Christ our Lord. Amen.   *(PW)*

The real presence

Once when Oda was celebrating the Eucharist, the heavenly Lamb comforted him with a marvellous miracle. After the reading of the holy Gospel, the offertory and the confession, Oda took up with his chaste hands the sacred mysteries, handling the bread, which signified the body of his faithful Friend and Redeemer. As he did this, he saw the ancient miracle being renewed at that moment.

There flowed a drop of blood from the true body of Christ, which he saw with his own eyes. He was awe-struck and filled with fear, and deeply troubled. He called a priest who was his friend, and showed him what was happening. Then by a prayer the form of the bread was reinstated as before, as he had first received it with tears and a contrite heart.

There and then, Oda ordered that all the poor, the wayfarers, the orphans and widows in Canterbury, should be assembled and provided with a solemn feast to mark so great a miracle.

(*Life of Oswald*)

BONIFACE

5 June

St Boniface is the best known of the many English
missionaries, men and women, who in the eighth century
took Christianity to the Low Countries and Germany.
Inspired by the example and encouragement of
his predecessor, Willibrord, Boniface sought the active support
of the papacy as a missionary and reformer of
the Frankish Church. His many letters give a vivid picture
of his activities and of his friends; he died as a martyr in Frisia
in 754, and is buried at Fulda in Germany.

O God, you have called the whole world to come to the knowledge of your truth by the preaching of your saints and teachers,
grant that by heeding their words, we may follow the example of
your blessed martyrs, St Boniface and his companions, and so
come to you. We ask this through Jesus Christ our Lord. Amen.

(PW)

O Author of boundless goodness and infinite mercy, who with
most certain proofs declared yourself to be both God and man.
You called your apostles, and taught them how to preach the
gospel, to cure people from all manner of diseases, to expel
demons and to raise the dead. I thank you, and humbly beg your
majesty to give me spiritual medicine for my body and soul, and
the power of your authority which will protect me intact from
all the assaults of my enemy. Awaken me by it from the sleep of
sin and the torpor of human laziness, and restore me from all
evil habits, O Lord Jesus Christ, Amen.   *(NNM)*

This magnificent 'Rupert Cross' is a fitting memorial to the impact of the English monasteries on Germany. It was created in the eighth century, probably by an English craftsman working on the Continent. Its style is very close to the Northumbrian art of this period, and it was associated with Bischofshofen, near Salzburg in Austria.

'We are of the same flesh and blood as you!'

We beg you, brethren, out of love to remember us in your prayers, that we may escape the opposition of the enemy and all assaults by evil men, so that the word of God may go forward and take root. We urge you to carry on praying that God and the Lord Jesus Christ, who desire the salvation of all by the knowledge of the Truth, may convert the hearts of the heathen Saxons to Christianity. May they reject the errors of paganism and become true children of the Church our mother. Take pity on them for they often say to us: 'We are of the same flesh and blood as you!' Remember also that after death and in hell none can praise or honour the Lord.

For this work I have received the encouragement and active support of two bishops of the Holy See of Rome. Please respond to my request for prayer, that your reward in heaven may be great in the presence of God's holy angels. So may God the almighty Creator preserve you in unity, and in the fellowship of his love forever.

(*Letter of Boniface: 738*)

Grant me, O Lord, true and surpassing love;
firmness of faith in my heart;
the helmet of salvation on my head;
the sign of the Christ on my forehead;
the word of salvation in my mouth;
a good will in my mind;
the girdle of chastity around my loins;
honesty in all I do;
sobriety in my way of life;
humility in prosperity;

patience in affliction;
hope in my Creator;
love of eternal life;
and perseverance until the end. Amen.

(NNM)

Preachers not predators

Faith is, as St Augustine teaches, born of will, not compulsion. A person can only be attracted into Christianity, he can never be forced. If he is forced to be baptised, it is useless for engendering true faith, except in a baby. An adult must be able to answer personally for his own beliefs and desires. To profess faith falsely is to prevent true salvation.

If the message of Christ and the burden of his light yoke were preached to the obdurate Saxons as keenly as demands for taxes and legal punishments are being imposed [i.e. by Charlemagne's government], perhaps they would not reject the whole idea of Christian baptism.

Teachers of Christianity must be educated in the example of the apostles. They must be preachers, not predators, trusting in the goodness of God alone. (Letter of Alcuin: 796)

Almighty and merciful God, have mercy upon me a sinner; grant me forgiveness from my sins, and freedom from all ills, for the honour of your name, and through the merits of your glorious and blessed apostles, the faith of your confessors, and the victories of your martyrs, who attained the heavenly crown for the sake of your name; also by the merits and prayers of your Catholic Church, which you have redeemed through the precious blood of your Son, and by the intercessions of all your saints who have pleased you since the foundation of the world. For you live and reign, God forever and ever. Amen. (*NNM*)

May God, who crowned with heavenly triumph his blessed martyr Boniface as he succumbed to the waves of his own blood, pour upon you the abundant grace of his blessing.

May he who joined him to the company of the angels by the torments of his suffering, grant you to become a companion of the heavenly citizens, by the effect of your good deeds; so that as you celebrate, while still in time, the feast of his holy martyr on earth, so by his prayers you may prove worthy to rejoice with him in glory forever. Amen. (*CB*)

Alban the Martyr

22 June

Although Alban died in the third century long before the coming of the Anglo-Saxons, his shrine was kept alive by the British Church after the Romans left in 410, and Bede took care to record the account of his martyrdom in his *History*. In the tenth century, the monastery at St Albans was reformed into a Benedictine community.

Be ready to hear us, O Lord God Almighty, and as you willed St
Alban your martyr and his companions to suffer in the same
storm of affliction in order to be adorned with the crown of
martyrdom, so may we with fitting devotion commemorate
their suffering, and sense the heavenly protection of their life
with you. We ask this through Jesus Christ our Lord. Amen.

(*PW*)

Noble Alban, fruitful Britain's son

*Alban sheltered a Christian priest fleeing persecution. As he saw
him at prayer, his heart was opened to the grace of God, and he
became instructed in the Christian faith. After a while, word got
out that a Christian fugitive was hiding in Alban's home. Soldiers
came and after a thorough search they found their man. But in fact
it was Alban dressed up in the priest's cloak.*

*When he saw who it was, the magistrate was furious. He com-
manded Alban to sacrifice to the gods. But Alban freely declared
that he was now a Christian. 'If you would like to know the truth
of my faith, realise that I am quite ready to do my duty as a
Christian!'*

*Blessed Alban was beheaded on 22 June near the Roman city of
Verulamium. Later when the Church was at peace, a lovely church
was built there as a memorial to his martyrdom. Even today many
sick people are healed there by the saint's miracles.*

(Bede - *History*)

Etheldreda of Ely

23 June

Etheldreda was an East Anglian princess, who, after her marriage to the King of Northumbria, relinquished her husband and founded a monastery at Ely in the fens. Seventeen years after her death in 679, her body was found to be incorrupt.

Almighty and eternal God, the author of virtue and lover of virginity, you deigned to lead blessed Etheldreda on this day to the joys of heaven. We humbly implore your mercy, that as we celebrate her sacred feast here on earth, we may rejoice in her benevolence among the stars. We ask this through Jesus Christ our Lord. Amen.   (*PW*)

A mother to heaven's king

Our age is crowned by its own glorious virgin, Etheldreda.
She sprang from royal stock, but found higher nobility in the
    service of God.
Her throne in heaven is more glorious than any on earth.
She sought no earthly husband having Christ as her
    Bridegroom.
Led by the Holy Mother, the Queen of heaven,
She became a mother to heaven's King.

(Bede)

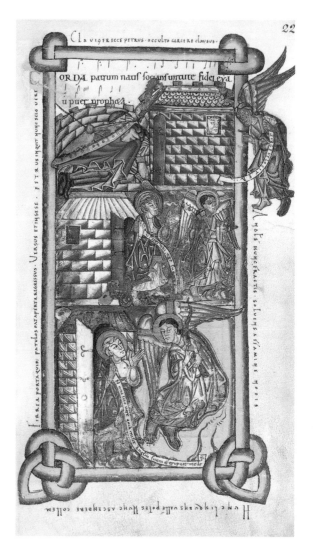

This picture of the release of St Peter from prison comes from the very end of the Anglo-Saxon period, in the later eleventh century. It appears in a book of liturgical music for festivals of the Church, called a Troper. Its style is derived from the Winchester school, though its place of origin is unknown.

ST PETER

29 June

Christianity came to England principally from Rome,
and the popes in their correspondence frequently appealed
to the spiritual authority of St Peter.
Many early English churches were dedicated to this saint,
and his authority was invoked to resolve
the correct calculation of Easter at the Synod
of Whitby in 664. Pilgrimage to Rome 'ad limina
apostolorum' enabled English kings and bishops
to draw close to the roots of Christianity
in the New Testament.

O God, you have consecrated your Church by the name and faith of your apostle St Peter, and have glorified blessed Paul with him in the evangelisation of the Gentiles. Grant that all who gather here to celebrate the feast of your apostles may be enriched with spiritual rewards. We ask this through Jesus Christ our Lord. Amen. (*PW*)

Lord God Almighty, you are wonderful in all your works, and you satisfied five thousand people with five loaves and two fish. I thank you, and pray that in accordance with this miracle you will grant to us sufficient strength in our weakness. May our minds be renewed by your salvation, that we may lead a devout way of life, and so receive with joy the action of your grace. We ask this through Jesus Christ our Lord. Amen. (*NNM*)

'The heavenly key-bearer who opens the gate of heaven'

Surely the Catholic faith and true harmony in Christian fellowship are inseparable? The implication is therefore clear: it is idle to boast of being a Catholic Christian unless you follow the teaching and authority of St Peter. The foundation of the Church and of our faith is fundamentally Christ himself; but it is also by delegation Peter as well.

Nor can this foundation ever be shaken by the blasts of hell. For St Paul teaches that there is no other foundation laid than that of Jesus Christ; and Christ himself as divine truth has established inviolable this privilege for Peter: 'You are Peter, and upon this rock I shall build my Church.'

(Aldhelm)

You, Lord, are almighty yet gentle, and full of mercy; you do not despise the contrite heart or the afflictions of the wretched. You revealed the depth of your kindness to blessed Peter the apostle after the bitter tears of his penitence. Show to me also the same compassion, lest I be cast out for my deserts, and separated from the friendship of your company. I beg your clemency most sincerely that, when lack of faith threatens me, your generous grace will meet me there, and in all its splendour forgive my many downfalls, and so give blessing to the wretched and unworthy, O Lord Jesus Christ. Amen.

(*NNM*)

Will the shepherd abandon the flock?

Laurence succeeded Augustine as Archbishop of Canterbury, but when King Ethelbert died there was a sharp reaction against the new faith. The Archbishop was planning to follow his fellow-bishops, Mellitus and Justus, in flight from Britain. That night he ordered his bed to be placed in the church of the holy apostles, Peter and Paul, and after many prayers and tears he fell asleep.

Suddenly in a dream there appeared to him the prince of the apostles, who scourged him long and hard in the darkness. St Peter challenged him severely as to why he proposed to abandon the flock entrusted to him, and to whom he would leave them at risk of attack. He reminded Laurence of his own sufferings as a martyr: 'In the end I endured death by crucifixion by the enemies of Christ that I might receive his crown.'

Next morning, deeply moved by this experience, the Archbishop went to the king and showed him the marks of the beating on his back. The king was astonished, and, when told what had happened, became afraid. He banned the worship of idols, gave up his unlawful wife, became a Christian and was baptised. He also sent messengers to Gaul to recall Mellitus and Justus from their exile, inviting them to return and to rule over their churches in freedom.

(Bede - *History*)

O Giver of wonderful divine medicine, who permitted your side to be pierced by a spear: open the gate of life to my knocking, that having entered thereby I may lay open to you all the wounds of my sins for healing by the medicine of your mercy, streaming from your wounded side. May I never receive complacently, for I am a debtor, the sacrament of your body and blood, given on account of my sins; but may my soul be filled with the abundance of your mercies, that he who is my ransom may also be my reward, even Jesus Christ my Lord. Amen.   (*NNM*)

May God, who constituted blessed Peter as prince of the apostles, and entrusted to him the keys of the kingdom of heaven and power over the gates of hell, grant to you absolution of your sins, and victory over all the assaults of your enemies.

May this most holy doorkeeper, whose shadow healed the sick, be a compassionate intercessor for you, for he excels as the shepherd of the Church after God himself. Amen.   (*CB*)

ST BENEDICT

11 July

The influence of St Benedict runs like a golden thread throughout Anglo-Saxon church history. He lived in Italy between 480 and 550, as a hermit and abbot, and distilled his spiritual teaching into a Rule for monastic community life. St Gregory the Great wrote up his life, and both *Rule* and *Life* became highly influential. The revival of monasticism in the tenth century sought to make the 'Rule of St Benedict' mandatory for all English monasteries by issuing the *Regularis Concordia* in 970.

Almighty and eternal God, you lifted up your blessed confessor Benedict on this day to heaven from the prison-house of the flesh. Grant us pardon from all our sins and may we your servants rejoice in heart at his glory, and sense his influence with you by his prayers. We ask this through Jesus Christ our Lord. Amen.   *(PW)*

Almighty and eternal God, you have set the radiant example of your confessor blessed Benedict before your servants as they pursue their arduous spiritual journey in his footsteps. May we so tread without error in the way of his teaching, that we may prove worthy to mingle with those who now rejoice in the land of the living. We ask this through Jesus Christ our Lord. Amen.

(PW)

Finding a spiritual father

Benedict Biscop charged his monks upon his deathbed never to appoint an abbot on grounds of birth or kinship. 'Always appoint from your own community, never from outside it. According to the Rule of St Benedict, our founder, and the privileges of this monastery, you are to meet to discern who is most worthy, by his teaching and example, to serve as abbot. You must choose only the best candidate after careful and compassionate scrutiny. Then you must ask the bishop to bless and confirm your choice.

Those who give birth to spiritual children by the Word of God must be guided by spiritual principles. Let the person most endowed with divine grace be regarded as the eldest son of the community, and let him be preferred above the rest for this office.

(Bede – *Lives of the Abbots*)

Almighty and merciful God, you caused blessed Benedict to depart to the glory of heaven in the sight of his disciples. Grant us also the help of the prayers of so outstanding a shepherd of monks, that, following his example and with his assistance, we may be worthy to attain to eternal life, through Jesus Christ our Lord. Amen.   (*PW*)

The Regularis Concordia

By the grace of our Lord Jesus Christ, we intend to maintain with all our power everything which has been handed down to us from our father Benedict, and which we have freely assumed for ourselves: measured amounts of food, clothing, fasting, ascetic discipline, and the virtue of obedience.

This picture shows St Benedict as the 'father of monks' instructing the monastery of Christ Church, Canterbury, where it was produced in the early eleventh century. It is part of a Psalter associated with a monk called Eadui, who appears as a kneeling figure at the feet of the saint, while his brethren hold up an open copy of the *Rule of St Benedict*.

In fulfilment of our covenant, and with the utmost care as far as we are able, and led by the prompting of the Holy Spirit, we shall now set forth clearly in writing all those customs surrounding the holy Rule, as they have been observed everywhere by the holy disciples of Benedict himself, after much careful reflection and experience.

We seek only to establish brotherly unity, with the advice of our king, and trusting in the commandments of those who have gone before us in this way of life. We pray that all who observe these monastic customs in a spirit of peace and gratitude may receive eternal life as a reward from him who makes men to be of one mind in a house, where God is the true king, even the Son of God, born of the holy Virgin, who with the Father and the Holy Spirit lives and reigns for ever. Amen.   (Prologue to the *Regularis Concordia*)

Lord God, the giver of all good gifts, look with favour upon your people as they celebrate this divine service in your honour. As we celebrate the passing of your holy confessor Benedict to blessedness, so may his example ever guide your Church. May his prayers establish within us true faith, an exemplary lifestyle, a chaste sobriety, loving hospitality, spiritual prudence, heavenly wisdom, a humble mind, and in the end eternal life. We ask this through Jesus Christ our Lord. Amen.   (*CB*)

Mildred of Thanet

13 July

Mildred became a nun at Minster-in-Thanet, and by 694 was
its Abbess, dying around the year 700. Her kindness towards
the sick and poor were long remembered, and her monastery
played an important role in supporting the mission of
St Boniface under the leadership of her successor, Eadburga.

Almighty and eternal God, show us your mercy as we pray; that
we who are uncertain of the quality of our own spiritual lives
may sense your forgiveness rather than your judgement, as a
result of the prayers of your blessed virgin, Mildred. We ask this
through Jesus Christ our Lord. Amen.   (*PW*)

The ties of spiritual friendship

To his dear sister, the abbess Eadburga, long united to him by spiri-
tual ties, Boniface, a servant of the servants of God, sends greetings
in Christ.
  May the Eternal Rewarder of all good works give heavenly joy
among the choirs of angels to my dearest sister, who has sent light
and comfort to an exile in Germany by sending him gifts of spiritual
books. No one can survive in these gloomy places serving the German
people unless the Word of God shines like a lamp about his path.
  I beg you of your love to pray for me, because as a punishment for
my sins I am being tossed around by the storms of this world. May
God remember me, that I may speak out boldly, so that the Word of
God may run with victory, and the gospel of Christ be glorified
among heathen people.   (Letter of Boniface)

Swithun of Winchester
15 July

**Little is known about Swithun's life and work,
and he died in 862. But during the revival of monasticism
in the tenth century his cult sprang to prominence in
Winchester, surrounded by many miracles,
and the cathedral was rebuilt to accommodate his shrine.**

O God, you caused your holy bishop Swithun to shine forth by many miracles to the glory of your Church. Grant us remission of our sins for the sake of his love of you, and fill us with all goodwill. May we after this life attain to Paradise, where your precious blood has prepared an eternal kingdom for all who truly love you. We ask this through Jesus Christ our Lord. Amen.

(*PW*)

Hidden but revealed

During the days of King Edgar, when by God's grace, Christianity was flourishing in England, God revealed St Swithun, confirming his sanctity by many miracles. Until this happened, he was virtually unknown, nor can we find out in books how this bishop lived while in this world, such was the carelessness of his contemporaries who failed to record what sort of man he was. All that was known was that Swithun had been a bishop of Winchester, and now lay buried outside the western end of the cathedral.

After several miracles at his tomb, King Edgar commanded that the saint be exhumed, and told Bishop Ethelwold to translate him

in great state into the cathedral. So Ethelwold, with accompanying
abbots and monks, solemnly took up the relics and carried them
with chanting into the church of St Peter, the Old Minster. There
they remain in great honour, working many miracles to this day.
On many occasions the burial-ground around the cathedral was so
full of crippled folk that they could scarcely get into the church.

(Aelfric – *Homily on Swithun*)

Ethelwold of Winchester

1 August

Ethelwold was a friend and contemporary of Dunstan,
and one of his disciples at Glastonbury. Around 950,
he created a strict Benedictine monastery at Abingdon,
and in 963 Dunstan made him Bishop of Winchester.
He introduced monks to the religious communities there,
and went on to found many monasteries
throughout England, notably Ely and Peterborough.

O God, on this day you caused new light to shine forth among the glorious stars of heaven for the English people in the brilliance of your holy bishop Ethelwold. We humbly beg your mercy that as we recognise his teaching and authority throughout our land, so we may be formed by his example and helped by his protection. We ask this through Jesus Christ our Lord. Amen.   (*PW*)

The mind of a reformer

I considered a translation of the Rule of St Benedict a very necessary thing. For it does not matter by which language someone is drawn to the faith, so long as in the end they come to God. So let those who only speak English observe it with no excuse! I beg all my successors in the name of our Lord to ensure that the observance of this holy Rule is increased by Christ's grace throughout our land, and many thereby be brought to spiritual perfection.

Let no man diminish the patrimony of God and so undermine the fire of holy religion as happened in the past when kings had little fear of God. Let us heed the warning and pray earnestly that the old state of affairs never returns. Let no abbot or abbess give away church lands for money or flattery. For they are set as God's shepherds and trustees. May the possessions granted to the Church remain in perpetuity, and may anyone who subverts this languish in the pains of hell!   (Ethelwold)

Oswald the Martyr

5 August

Oswald was the young king of Northumbria who invited
St Aidan to come as a missionary, and to found
the monastery on Lindisfarne. He was the bishop's interpreter
during the early stages of the mission.
He was a warlike ruler who died fighting in 642.
He was regarded as a royal martyr. There is an account of
the decisive battle at the beginning of his reign among
the readings on the Cross.

Almighty and eternal God, you consecrated this joyful and blessed day in honour of your holy servant Oswald. Give us such an increase of fear and love in our hearts, that as we celebrate on earth the shedding of his sacred blood, so we may sense his protection of our hearts and minds. We ask this through Jesus Christ our Lord. Amen. *(PW)*

'May this hand never decay!'

Although Oswald exercised unparalleled power, he remained amazingly kind, humble and generous to the poor. Once, on Easter day, as he sat at dinner with Bishop Aidan, a silver plate full of food was placed before them. Just as they were about to say grace, a servant whose duty it was to assist those in need came in, and told the king that there was a great crowd of poor folk outside his hall.

The king immediately ordered that all the special food be carried out to them, and that the silver dish should be broken up into small pieces and shared among them. The bishop was astonished at such charity, and grasping his right hand, declared: 'May this hand never decay!'

In fact, after his martyrdom, the bishop's prayer was fulfilled, for this part of the king's body remains incorrupt, and it is preserved and venerated in the royal fortress at Bamburgh.   (Bede - *History*)

Aidan of Lindisfarne

31 August

Aidan came from St Columba's monastery on Iona at the invitation of King Oswald of Northumbria, to evangelise and to create the monastery on Lindisfarne. Bede describes him lovingly in his *History* as a model bishop - humble, sincere and fearless.

O God, you have raised a dwelling-place for your eternal majesty using the living and choice stones which are your saints. Help your people as they pray, that your Church may be enlarged physically in such a way that it may grow spiritually. We ask this through Jesus Christ our Lord. Amen.   (*PW*)

This child of God

The king gave Bishop Aidan a first-class horse to help him get across rivers, or to respond to some urgent need. Aidan's practice was normally to walk everywhere, and sometime later he met a beggar who asked for his help. Without a second thought, Aidan got off and gave him the horse with all its royal harness, for he was unfailingly kind and generous to the destitute.

The king heard of this, and as they were going in for a meal he accosted him: 'My Lord Bishop, why have you given away our royal horse which was intended for your use? We have many less valuable beasts, which would have been good enough for a poor man. And I chose that one specially for you!'

Aidan replied without any hesitation: 'My Lord King, what are you saying? Surely this foal of a mare is not more valuable to you than this child of God?'

They went in to eat, and the bishop sat down while the king warmed himself with his soldiers in front of the fire. Suddenly he recalled the bishop's rebuke. He threw down his sword, and ran and knelt at the bishop's feet to beg forgiveness: 'I will never judge how you use my money in the care of God's children!'

(Bede – *History*)

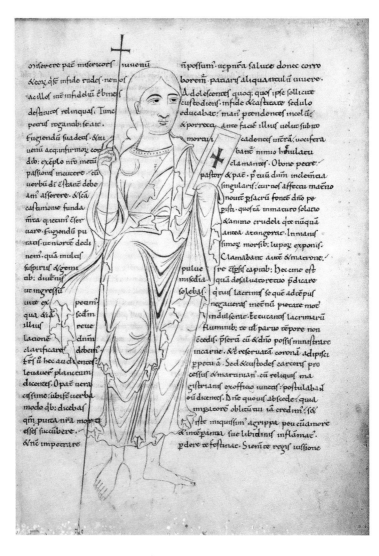

This powerful line drawing of Christ originates from Canterbury during the time of
St Dunstan. The meaning of the gospel of Christ is mediated through the words of
St Gregory's *Pastoral Care*. This work exerted permanent influence upon the ethos of the
Anglo-Saxon church, and was translated into English by King Alfred the Great.

GREGORY THE GREAT

3 September

St Gregory's spiritual vision and authority lay behind
the Roman mission to Kent in 597, and continued
to inspire and guide many generations of Anglo-Saxon
Christians. The first life of the saint was composed
by an unknown monk at Whitby, and Bede regarded
himself as a disciple of Gregory in his work
of expounding the Bible. English missionaries to
the Continent in the eighth century also looked back
to his example and teaching, and his influence moulded
the ethos of the English Church throughout
the Anglo-Saxon centuries.

O God, who granted the prize of eternal blessedness to your servant Gregory, mercifully grant that we, who deserve to be
weighed for our sins, may by his prayers be uplifted to you. We
ask this through Jesus Christ our Lord. Amen.   (*PW*)

O God, you gave to your beloved Gregory such eminence and
authority that he became a column of light in your Church. He
served as a pillar of faith to your faithful people, and shone forth
as the apostle of the English. Clothe us in the brightness of his
gifts, that we may rejoice in the forgiveness of all our sins. We
ask this through Jesus Christ our Lord. Amen.   (*CB*)

'Not Angles but angels!'

It is said that before Gregory became pope, some of our own race appeared in Rome, fair of skin and hair. Gregory spotted them on sale as slaves. He asked their race, and was told that they were Angles. 'Not Angles, but angels!' he declared.

He was so moved by their plight and the spiritual opportunity it presented that he begged his predecessor, Pope Benedict, for permission to set out as a missionary to their land. 'It would be a wretched tragedy if hell were to be filled by such attractive people.' The Pope agreed, but the people of Rome prevented Gregory's departure from their city in its time of need. (*First Life of Gregory*)

Lord God the Ruler Almighty, you are One and Trinity, the Father in the Son and the Son in the Father, with the Holy Spirit. You are always in all things, you were before all things, and you will be beyond all things, God, blessed forever. I commend my soul into your powerful hands, that you may protect me day and night, moment by moment.

Have mercy upon me, O God, for I am an unworthy and unhappy person. Who can liberate me from this body of sin and death, unless it be the grace of our Lord Jesus Christ? I am not worthy to be called your servant: kindle within me the fire of your fear. Free my soul, and preserve me in your will. Teach me to do your will, for you are my God, to whom be honour and glory forever. Amen. (Attributed to Gregory in *NNM*)

The apostle of the English

To all his holy deeds should be added this fact, that it was he who rescued our people from the jaws of the enemy and enabled them to share in eternal freedom by sending missionaries to us. In these words, written in his commentary on the book of Job, he celebrates their courage and faith:

'The mouths of the British have learnt how to sing the praises of God, using the "Alleluias" of the Hebrews. The wild and proud ocean has become God's servant, submissive before His saints. Where earthly rulers were unable to conquer with the sword, the Word and fear of God prevail through the lips of priests. The unbeliever, brave before all who attacked him, now as a Christian respects the words of humble preachers. The Word of God with accompanying miracles has filled him with divine grace and understanding. Fear of the Lord now rules him so that he dreads evil and longs for eternal blessing.' By these words, Gregory indicates that St Augustine and his companions won over the English both by preaching and by miracles.

Meanwhile in Rome, Pope Gregory commanded that the Eucharist should be regularly celebrated in the churches where the apostles Peter and Paul lie buried. Into the words of celebration he inserted three petitions of great perfection: 'Grant us peace in our day, command that we be rescued from eternal condemnation, and number us among the company of your chosen ones.'

(Bede - *History*)

Almighty and merciful God, you deign to use the ministry of priests to serve you and pray to you. Of your great mercy grant that wherever we visit, you will visit with us, and whatever we bless you will bless. May our going out in all humility secure the flight of demons by the merits of your saints, and the entry of your angel of peace. We ask this through Jesus Christ our Lord. Amen.   (*PW*)

Lord Jesus Christ, who by entering Jerusalem hallowed its gates, and foreordained by the splendour of its twelve gems the names of your apostles; you proclaimed through prophecy in the psalms: 'Praise the Lord, O Jerusalem: praise thy God, O Zion. For he hath made fast the bars of thy gates: and hath blessed thy children within thee.' We ask you to place your peace in this church. May your Word run swiftly within it, full of nurture to satisfy all who enter it. May your Holy Spirit defend them, that no enemy may ever hurt them. May all who dwell within it sing with heart and mind: 'Great is our Lord Jesus Christ, and great is his virtue, and his wisdom is beyond fathoming, for he lives and reigns as God forever.' Amen.   (*PW*)

Birinus of Dorchester

4 September

Birinus was sent by Pope Honorius as a missionary to England. He arrived in 635 and worked among the West Saxons, with the support of their king, Cynegils. The King's daughter married Oswald of Northumbria, and Birinus baptised the King of Wessex with Oswald as sponsor. The centre of his mission was at Dorchester-on-Thames, but in 690 his relics were transferred to the new cathedral at Winchester.

O God, you have caused us to celebrate on this solemn day the feast of the translation of your confessor and bishop Birinus. Look with favour upon us, that his help for us may prevail in your presence, by whose holy preaching we have come to recognise the author of eternal salvation, even Jesus Christ our Lord. Amen.   *(PW)*

The baptism of a king

In the course of his preaching mission among the West Saxons, the king himself began to be instructed in Christianity, and came for baptism with many of his people. King Oswald of Northumbria was also present, and became his godfather. Their friendship was pleasing to God, and it was sealed by Oswald marrying the king's daughter, although the king was Oswald's spiritual son.

The two kings endowed Bishop Birinus with the town of Dorchester as a secure base for his cathedral and his mission. He was buried there after converting many to the Lord and dedicating many new churches. Much later, when Haedde was bishop, his remains were translated to the cathedral of St Peter and St Paul in Winchester.   (Bede – *History*)

THE BIRTH OF
THE BLESSED VIRGIN MARY
8 September

Devotion to St Mary runs throughout
the Anglo-Saxon period, culminating in art of
a profoundly contemplative nature in the tenth century.
The English Church was unusual in the West in celebrating
at this time the feasts of the presentation of the Virgin
in the temple and her conception, as well as those
of her birth and her repose. This was probably due to
Greek influence in the seventh century, perhaps
during the time of Archbishop Theodore of Tarsus.

Almighty and eternal God, who on this day revealed by the
ministry of an angel the coming of your co-eternal Son to be
conceived by the Holy Spirit in the flesh of blessed Mary, ever-
virgin, for the salvation of the world: attend kindly to the
prayers of your people, that we may run with freer hearts to celebrate his nativity in peace. We ask this through Jesus Christ our
Lord. Amen.   (*PW*)

Holy Mary, glorious Mother of God and ever-virgin, who was
worthy to bear the salvation of humanity, and to receive the glorious light of the world from heaven, which came to those sitting in darkness and in the shadow of death: be my loving lady
and the light of my heart, and my helper with God the almighty
Father. May I come to receive my heart's desire and, evading the
shadows of the underworld, be made worthy to attain to eternal
life. I ask this through Jesus Christ my Lord. Amen.   (*NNM*)

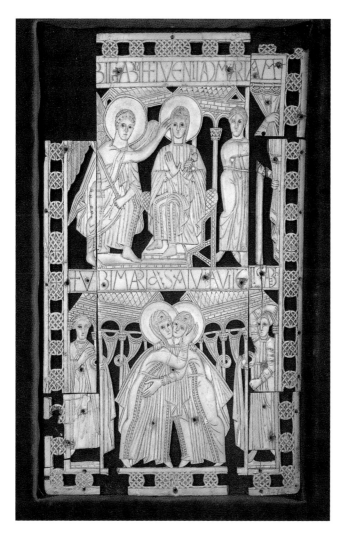

This elegantly and exquisitely carved ivory panel was part of a ceremonial book cover. It portrays the Annunciation to the Blessed Virgin Mary, and her Visitation to Elizabeth. The imperial setting and style reflect Byzantine influence, probably from Ravenna, and the eyes are set with bright blue glass. It was probably made by an English craftsman in the pre-Carolingian period in the eighth century, working in southern Germany or perhaps at Salzburg.

The joys of a life so lovely

On the feasts when the Virgin Mary blessed the celebration of her assumption into heaven, or the day of her birth as God's gift to this present age, or when she first received the joys of a life so lovely, or bore within herself the presence of God most high, the church was resplendent with holy joy.

Abbot Sigbald would sing from his heart out of love for Christ, with tears streaming down his face, and urge his monks with all gentleness and prayers to celebrate these solemn festivals in honour of so holy a mother.   (Ethelwulf – *De Abbatibus*)

Christ, suffering on the cross,
Hidden in the dark embrace of death,
As a virgin commended his virgin mother
To another virgin [i.e. St John] for her protection.

(Aldhelm)

The sweet love of Christ

When he was in residence in Canterbury, Dunstan used to visit the holy places in the dead of night to sing psalms and to keep vigil. On one occasion he moved to the eastern end of the church to pray to the Mother of God.

Suddenly and in a quite unexpected way he heard unusually sweet voices singing in the darkness, echoing through the church with subtle melodies. Peeping through a hole in the perforated screen, he saw that the church was completely filled with shining light, and a crown of virgins were moving round in procession, singing as a choir the hymn by the poet Sedulius: 'Cantemus socii Domino'.

Each half of the choir answered the other, verse by verse as if in a round, singing: 'Let us sing, O friends, let us sing to the honour of the Lord: let the sweet love of Christ sound through pious lips.'

(*First Life of Dunstan*)

O Lord, this feast day signifies for us an eternal mystery, whereby the holy Mother of God overcame temporal death, unoppressed by the bonds of mortality, for she had borne your incarnate Son, our Lord. We now seek his intercession, that we too may be able to escape the death of our souls. We ask this through Jesus Christ our Lord. Amen. (*PW*)

Almighty God, through the incarnation of your only-begotten Word you gave light to our age. We implore his mercy, that those whom he has drawn to new life within the flock of your holy Church may be absolved from all heathen error. Preserve your Church in your mercy with your heavenly protection, that your servants may ever remain steadfast. Grant that we who devoutly celebrate today the birth of your most holy Virgin and God-bearer may by her prayers be led, after laying down this burden of flesh, to the joys of your eternal kingdom. We ask this through Jesus Christ our Lord. Amen. (*CB*)

Theodore of Tarsus

19 September

Theodore was sent from Rome by Pope Vitalian in 666
to lead the English church after most of its bishops had been
wiped out by plague. He was aged sixty-five, and was
a Greek from Tarsus in Cilicia; he was also a monk and
theologian. He came with an African abbot, Hadrian,
and together they created a strong educational centre
at Canterbury. Theodore reorganised the English Church,
and died in 690.

O God, you have created an eternal home into which you gather
your saints from far and wide. Give your heavenly increase to
your Church, that as we embrace their relics here in pious love,
so we may ever be assisted by their prayers. We ask this through
Jesus Christ our Lord. Amen.   (*PW*)

A light yoke

*A person who would receive the Eucharist should make confession
first, and the priest ought to consider the age and education of the
person, and what is appropriate to them. Priestly authority is to be
moderated in proportion to infirmity, and this principle applies to
all penance and confession: what will most enable God to help
people, and what may be obeyed by them in all diligence?*

(Theodore's *Penitential*)

Lioba of Bischofsheim

28 September

**Lioba was one of the many noble English women
attracted to the mission-field in Germany during
the eighth century. She was a younger contemporary
and personal friend of Boniface, with whom
she corresponded. She came from the monastery
in Thanet, and joined Boniface in 748.
She founded and presided over a convent at Bischofsheim,
and died in 782, when she was buried with Boniface at Fulda.**

O God, the lover of justice and hater of iniquity, you delight in
looking upon the glory of virginity in its beauty. Pour upon us
the fullness of virtue in response to the prayers of your holy virgins, that we may run with joy after the love of your delights,
which are found in our Saviour, Jesus Christ our Lord. Amen.

(PW)

Beloved in Christ

*To the most reverend Boniface, dearly beloved in Christ and related
to me by kinship, the lowest of the handmaids of Christ sends
warmest wishes for eternal joy.*

*I am my parents' only child, and would like to regard you as my
brother, for there is no other man in my family in whom I can put
my trust as I can in you. I am sending you this little gift so that you
may always remember me with a bond of true affection. May your
prayers shield me from all temptations. Can you also correct the*

style of my letter and write back to me, for I long to hear from you again?

I have composed this small poem: can you correct this also? I learnt how to do so from my mistress, Abbess Eadburga, who continues her study of the Bible with great diligence.

> *Eternal Ruler, the sole Creator of all things,*
> *You fill with light your Father's kingdom.*
> *May the glory of Christ shine forth in power,*
> *Prevailing inexorably by your eternal command.*

(Letter of Lioba to Boniface)

MICHAELMAS

29 September

Angels feature prominently in Anglo-Saxon art and sculpture,
and also in the lives of saints. In the earliest lives,
Irish influence may be detected, for Irish missionaries
brought with them the memory of St Columba of Iona who
frequently encountered angels. Many ancient church
dedications, on sites of former pagan shrines
and high places, were to St Michael, the prince of the angels;
and the sense of spiritual conflict with evil is seldom absent
from the remaining religious writing.

Grant us, Almighty God, so to advance the honour of the
Archangel Michael, that as we proclaim his glory on earth, so his
prayers may assist us in heaven. We ask this through Jesus Christ
our Lord. Amen.   *(PW)*

St Michael the Archangel, you come to the help of God's people:
plead for me with the most high Judge that he may give to me, a
sinner, remission of all my sins, for the sake of your great mercy
and forbearance. Hear me, St Michael, as I call upon you; help
me as I sigh to you. Make me clean from all my sins.

I beg you also to exercise your noble and eminent ministry
before the most high God, that on the last day you will receive
my soul kindly into your embrace, and lead me to a place of
refreshment, light and peace, where the souls of the saints rest,
and wait with joy and unceasing gladness for the future judgement and blessed resurrection. I ask this through him who lives
and reigns as God forever. Amen.   *(NNM)*

Angels feature prominently in the art and sculpture of the later Anglo-Saxon period. This beautiful and ethereal figure comes from a Gospel-book, now in Oxford, in which angels, rather than portraits of the evangelists, preface each gospel. This one precedes the gospel of St Luke, in which angels play a crucial role.

Entertaining angels unawares

Once when Cuthbert was serving as a monk at Ripon, he was responsible for the care of guests coming to the monastery. Early one day, in mid-winter when snow lay on the ground, an angel'of the Lord appeared in the form of a man, even as the angels appeared to Abraham at Mamre.

Cuthbert received him kindly as usual, washing and rubbing his feet with towels and also with his own hands to warm them up. He invited him in and urged him to wait until nine o'clock in the morning when food would be served. But he declined and wanted to move on with his journey. In the end Cuthbert persuaded him to wait in the name of our Lord Jesus Christ.

But when the time came there were only a few crumbs of bread for the table. So Cuthbert went across to the monastery to find a loaf of bread, but they were still baking it. So Cuthbert returned to his guest empty-handed. He had left him alone, but he discovered that his visitor had gone. To his astonishment there were no foot-prints in the snow! Cuthbert realised that it had been an angel of God, and as he removed the table back to the storeroom he smelt some hot bread, and found there three warm loaves.

(*First Life of Cuthbert*)

I believe that you are the holy angel sent by almighty God to protect me. I therefore implore you in all humility, and for the sake of him who thus commanded you, to guard me, a weak, wretched and unworthy person, always and everywhere in the course of my life. Protect and defend me from all harm, and when God orders my soul to depart from here, let no demonic power be permitted to detain me, but rather may you receive my soul from my body in gentleness. Lead me smoothly to the bosom of Abraham by the command and help of our Creator and Saviour, God who is blessed forever. Amen.

(*Hyde Liber Vitae*)

Music from heaven

One night after his prayers and the completion of the divine office, Dunstan was falling asleep when he had a vision of heaven. He saw his own mother, who had died, joined in marriage to a high king. There was a great company singing with joy the sweetest hymns.

A young man, dressed in white, came up to him and asked him why he was not joining in the singing. Dunstan replied that he knew no suitable songs for such an occasion. The angel asked him: 'Do you wish me to teach you how you ought to sing?' Dunstan agreed with all humility. So he was taught this antiphon:

'O King of the nations and Ruler of all things, from the throne of your majesty grant us, O Christ our King, forgiveness of all our sins: Alleluia!'

This was repeated to him so often that it became embedded in his memory, arousing within him a sighing murmur as he recalled it. Dunstan ordered it to be preserved, and it was noted down in the morning by one of the monks at his dictation. Whenever the monks came later to sing it, Dunstan was always moved to tears, declaring that his vision of the angel had indeed been real and true.

(*First Life of Dunstan*)

Almighty and eternal God, in the beginning you willed into existence the heavens, the angels and all celestial powers. You gave them intelligence, and granted them intimately to contemplate you. You endowed them with all knowledge, and made them possessors and citizens of your holy kingdom, to persist in all goodness. As a holy ruler you granted them the purest gift, that none of them would choose or be able to sin. I lay hold of these acts of your grace, and beg you, the author of such immense goodness, that you will confirm me in the same fear of you that they enjoy. For you are their strength and stay above lest they fall: generously regard me here below, and be my true helper, so that after falling I may arise, O Lord God of hosts. Amen.   (*NNM*)

May the Lord richly bless you who meet today to celebrate the feast of St Michael, prince of the archangels: may the joy of his merits fill the whole world.

May he, who this day triumphed over the ancient enemy, enable you to overcome with his helps the assaults of the same dragon.

May God in the end receive your souls into eternal rest, that you may join in the singing choirs of the angels in perpetual exultation. Amen.   (*CB*)

Paulinus of York

10 October

**Paulinus came as one of the second group of missionaries
sent by Pope Gregory in 601. When Edwin of Northumbria
married a Christian princess from Kent, Paulinus went north
as her bishop. After lengthy deliberation, the king and
his family finally became Christian in 628, and were baptised
by Paulinus in York. His missionary work continued until
Edwin's death in battle in 633. He fled south and ended his days
as Bishop of Rochester in 644.**

Most merciful Father and Lord God Almighty, we thank you
continually for our teacher, Paulinus, who came to us through
St Gregory's initiative, although we were not able to receive him
in person. At the very close of his life you revealed him as one
truly faithful to you, for some saw his soul depart to heaven in
the form of a beautiful swan. Hear our prayer through Jesus
Christ our Lord. Amen.   (*First Life of Gregory*)

Venerable and awe-inspiring

*A certain abbot told me personally of how Christianity came to our
kingdom. An old man had once described to him how he had been
baptised in the river Trent at midday by Bishop Paulinus along
with many others, in the presence of King Edwin.*

*He described Paulinus as tall with a slight stoop; he had black hair,
a thin face, a slender aquiline nose, and was striking because of his
venerable and awe-inspiring appearance. There was a deacon help-
ing him, called James, a missionary of great energy and Christ-like
character, who was still living in our own times.*   (Bede – *History*)

Ethelburga of Barking

11 October

Ethelburga was sister to Erkenwald, Bishop of London,
and ruled as abbess over the convent they had founded
at Barking. Bede recounts her sanctity at some length
in his *History*, and her community attracted
the respect of Aldhelm and Boniface during the rule
of her successor, Hildelith. Aldhelm's work *De Virginitate*
was dedicated to the nuns of Barking.

O God, you draw virgins after you: draw us also in your unfailing kindness, and present us with your holy virgins in the palace
of the great King, Jesus Christ our Lord. Amen.   (*PW*)

Stricken by plague

*The mother of the community, Ethelburga, was full of anxiety,
wondering who would be struck down next by the plague, which
was sweeping the land. She called the sisters together to ask them
where they wanted a cemetery cleared to receive their bodies. She
could get no clear decision, such was their fear.*

*One night not long after, as they were processing through the
monks' graveyard singing psalms, a great light appeared from
heaven and filled them with alarm. It moved across to the southern
side of the monastery, to the west of the chapel. There it remained
for some time until it faded. They took it as a sign to guide them to
heaven, and to indicate the place of their burial.* (Bede – *History*)

James the Deacon
11 October

**James probably came with the missionaries from Italy,
and was the companion of Paulinus during his missionary
episcopate in Northumbria during the reign of King Edwin.
James stayed on after Paulinus had fled to Kent,
and survived until after the Synod of Whitby in 664.**

Almighty and eternal God, you have founded your Church upon
the foundation of the apostles, and have thrown down with
terror the gates of hell. Enable us to persevere in proclaiming
your truth, that we may have no truck with evil. We ask this
through Jesus Christ our Lord. Amen.   (*PW*)

A faithful servant

*Paulinus left James at York after his departure to Kent. He was a
deacon, truly dedicated to the Church and of saintly character. He
remained for many years there, teaching the faith and baptising
the people, snatching them from their evil ways.*

*He was also a skilled church musician, and when peace returned
to Northumbria, he was able to revive the art of singing in church,
in the style which prevailed in Kent and at Rome. He died peace-
fully, full of years.*   (Bede – *History*)

Wilfrid of Ripon

12 October

Wilfrid was one of the first generation of English bishops,
who was educated at Lindisfarne. In 653 he went to Rome,
and on his return became Abbot of Ripon, where
he introduced the Rule of St Benedict. He played a key role
at the Synod of Whitby in 664 in favour of the Roman way of
calculating Easter. By 669 he was Bishop of York,
but by 680 had fallen out with the king and with
Archbishop Theodore. He made several visits to Rome
to plead his cause, acting as missionary in Frisia
and Sussex in between; he died in 709.

Grant us, O Lord, to cease from all distraction by this world as a
result of the prayers of your blessed confessor and bishop
Wilfrid. May his help and protection in this present life enable
us to attain to the reward of your eternal blessedness. We ask this
through Jesus Christ our Lord. Amen.   *(PW)*

'I appeal to Rome!'

*'Why do you persist in persecuting me and forcing me to condemn
myself? Shall I scandalise those who know me, seeing that I have
served now as a bishop for over forty years?*

*Was I not the first, after the death of the missionaries sent by St
Gregory, to root out the poisonous weeds planted by the Irish
monks? Did I not convert the whole of Northumbria to the correct
celebration of Easter and the Roman mode of tonsure? Did I not*

teach them how to sing properly, using a double choir, singing reciprocal antiphons and responses in harmony? Did I not order monastic life for the first time according to the Rule of St Benedict?

Do you really expect me now to condemn myself in order to fall in with your plans, and so violate my sacred office as bishop? I appeal again to the Apostolic See, and challenge anyone here to go with me there to secure judgement! Let the wisdom of Rome decide!'   (*Life of Wilfrid*)

Edward the Confessor

13 October

**Edward was the last of the Anglo-Saxon kings,
and his death in 1066 precipitated the crisis, which led to
the Norman invasion. He was a devout ruler,
remembered for his compassion and humility, and
Westminster Abbey was built at his behest,
and is his burial-place. This promise was placed
at the start of the coronation service by Dunstan in 973.**

O God, you have crowned your blessed confessor King Edward with eternal glory: teach us so to respect his example on earth,

that we may be enabled to reign with him in heaven. We ask this
through Jesus Christ our Lord. Amen.   (Traditional)

The promise of a king

*In the name of the Holy Trinity, I promise three things to the
Christian people, my subjects:*

*First, that God's Church and all Christian people within my
dominions shall experience true peace.*

*Second, that I forbid robbery and all crime to every class of
people.*

*Third, I promise and order laws based on justice and mercy,
that the gracious and merciful God may forgive us all our sins.*

*The duty of a Christian king is to judge no one corruptly, to
defend widows, orphans and strangers, and to abolish immoral
marriages. He must drive out those who practice magic, and who
murder their kin, or commit perjury. He must feed the needy, and
have old and experienced men for his counsellors, appointing
honest servants. He will be answerable on the Day of Judgement for
the crimes of his servants done in his name.*   (*Coronation Order*)

Frideswide of Oxford

19 October

Little is definitely known about Frideswide, who is traditionally believed to have escaped the clutches of a noble suitor, and to have made her life as a recluse at Binsey near Oxford. She later founded a monastery where Christ Church cathedral now stands.

O God, you endued blessed Frideswide with zeal for your Church and charity towards your people. Mercifully grant that we, who commemorate her life of holiness and self-denial, may be fruitful in all good works, and attain by your grace to the reward of the poor in spirit, the merciful, and the pure in heart. We ask this through Jesus Christ our Lord. Amen.   (Traditional)

Blessed are the pure in heart

Every blessing of pure virginity is preserved only in the fastness of a free mind, rather than in the more limited state of being physically intact. Enforced imposition upon the body can never undermine the blessing secured by an unshakeable free will.

St Augustine confirms this most elegantly when he declares: 'the sanctity of the body remains if the sanctity of the soul is intact, even when the body is overcome. Equally the sanctity of the body is lost if the purity of the soul is surrendered, even if the body remains physically intact.' Elsewhere he says that 'virginity of the heart is an unsullied faith'.   (Aldhelm – *On Virginity*)

Alfred the Great

26 October

Alfred died in 899, after an eventful reign.
In 878 he defeated the Vikings at the battle of Edington.
He went on to recapture London in 885, and to establish
a defensive strategy by land and sea to contain
the Viking threat. He laid the foundations for
the later success of Wessex in regaining the Danelaw
and creating the first united kingdom of the English.
He was also active in the revival of Christian culture and
monastic life, learning to read and write and to translate.

May the Lord, who has instructed me, cause me to abide more securely within this temporary dwelling-place, and also finally in the eternal homeland he has promised us through the writings of the holy fathers Augustine, Gregory, Jerome and many others. By their prayers, may he make my path easier before my face, and illumine the eyes of my mind, so that I may find the most direct way to the eternal glory and rest of his saints. May he permit me to be useful here, and to arrive safely there, through Jesus Christ his Son, our Lord. Amen.

(Alfred – *Preface to The Soliloquies*)

The collapse of learning

Once people sought wisdom and learning from this country; now we have to look for it abroad. Learning so collapsed in England that few there were on this side of the river Humber who could even understand the service in church, let alone translate a letter from English into Latin. I cannot actually recall a single name from south of the Thames when I began to rule.

Thank God that has now been remedied! So I implore you to free yourself as often as you can to apply yourself to seeking the wisdom of God. Remember how we were punished for our failure to transmit learning or to value it. Then we were Christians in name only, unable to possess the fullness of Christian virtue.

(Alfred – *Preface to The Pastoral Rule*)

Cedd of Lastingham
26 October

Cedd was one of three brothers educated at Lindisfarne
by Aidan and his companions. They became part of
the first generation of English priests and bishops.
Cedd was an evangelist in Mercia and then in Essex,
where he became its first bishop. He also founded the
monastery at Lastingham in Yorkshire, and was
an interpreter at the Synod of Whitby.
He died soon after in 664.

O God, the unfailing light of your saints, we beg you to extend to us the gifts of your blessing, and to remove all our sins in response to the prayers of Saint Cedd. May we be enrolled with him as inheritors of the joys of heaven. We ask this through Jesus Christ our Lord. Amen. (PW)

The founding of Lastingham

The King of Northumbria realised that Cedd was a wise, holy and good man, and he offered him land on which to build a monastery which he could visit when he came to the kingdom from Essex, and where he might be buried.

Cedd personally chose the site for the new monastery. It was in the midst of steep and remote moors more suitable to the haunt of robbers or the dens of wild beasts. He spent the whole of Lent there in prayer and fasting to consecrate it to the Lord, according to Irish custom. He created there with his brothers a monastery in the tradition of Lindisfarne. (Bede – *History*)

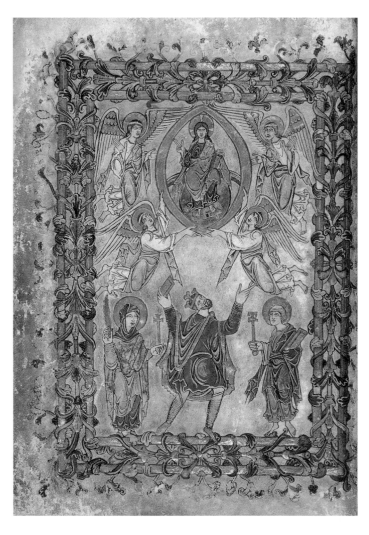

This powerful picture heralds the solemn gilded charter by which King Edgar endowed
the New Minster at Winchester as a reformed monastery in 966. It is the first fully
developed example of the Winchester school. Edgar's patronage was crucial in the
widespread creation and reform of the monasteries by Dunstan and Ethelwold.
The king offers the charter in the form of a book to Christ Himself, witnessed by
saints and angels.

ALL SAINTS

1 November

**This feast spread throughout the Western Church during
the Anglo-Saxon period. Its origin was the consecration of
the Pantheon in Rome as a church in 609, and it was promoted
by popes in the eighth and ninth centuries.
The English scholar, Alcuin, played a part in its dissemination.
Anglo-Saxon churches were richly decorated with icons
and frescos and other visual representations of
the communion of the saints, communicating the sense
of a living spiritual past giving life and depth to worship.**

Grant we beseech you, Almighty God, that the intercession of
Mary, the holy Mother of God, and all the blessed powers of
heaven, of the holy patriarchs, prophets, apostles, martyrs, confessors and virgins, and all your chosen people, may always gladden our hearts, and that while we reflect on their glory may we
sense their fellowship. We ask this through Jesus Christ our
Lord. Amen.   (*PW*)

O God, the Father of your blessed and beloved Son Jesus Christ,
through whom we have received knowledge of you, the God of
the angels and Creator and ruler of all things, visible and invisible: I offer heartfelt thanks to you, O God, that you have shown
such unmerited generosity and kindness to me, a wretched
sinner, and to my people and to all manner of human beings.

All creation praises you for you have created everything, and
through your will they exist. Therefore I too praise you in all

things, and for all things. I bless and glorify you forever as God
our supreme ruler, and Jesus Christ your beloved Son; through
whom and with whom be glory to you and to the Holy Spirit,
now and forever. Amen.   (Attributed to Augustine in *NNM*)

Sigbald's church

*Sigbald the abbot built a church worthy of God, in honour of the
holy Mother and for her indwelling beneath the sky. At its heart is
an altar, set about by wonderful paintings, and dressed in gems
and yellow gold, and faced with shining silver reliefs engraved with
figures: for bright indeed are the souls of the saints and their heavenly dwelling-places. It is crowned with flowers when the holy Gift
is placed in its pyx.*

*Painted on the western end of the church are the resplendent
angels, God's servants who fill heaven with beautiful music. All the
saints hover along the middle level of the church, filling it with
their presence at all times. They descend like snow in response to
the prayers of the faithful, and they defend them always by their
holy merits as they press forward to receive the palm of eternal life.*

*The church is full of lights overhead, which shine to our delight
and joy. There is a gleaming golden chalice, which Sigbald consecrated to the holy Mother: it is covered in precious stones, and is
etched in silver, which catches the light. The roof is protected with
lead, and copper bells are rung by the brethren in sweet music.*

(Ethelwulf)

God most high and God of mercy, who alone are without sin,
grant to me a sinner trust in the final hour because of your
manifold mercies, that my wickedness, which now lies concealed, may not be revealed before the awaiting angels and

archangels, the prophets and apostles, and other righteous and holy saints. But save me in your gracious compassion and mercy. Lead me into the paradise of your delights with all your perfect ones. Receive this request of your servant by the prayers of all your saints who have pleased you throughout the ages. For to you is due all adoration and glory, now and forever. Amen.

(NNM)

The true Temple

The division of the Temple in the Old Testament signifies a profound mystery. The outer part is the present Church where daily sacrifice of praise is offered to God. But the inner part represents the promised life of heaven, which indeed pre-exists this earthly life of our exile. There is celebrated, in the presence of God himself, that perpetual solemnity of the blessed, both angels and saints.

The altar of incense, which stood in the outer part of the Temple, but very close to the doorway into its inner sanctuary, represents the altar of the heart of holy men and women, who while detained in this life are still uplifted to the things of heaven by their heart's desire. Set on fire with heavenly love, their prayers ascend to the ears of God, like incense into the Holy of Holies. The purer their lives are on earth, the closer they live to their heavenly homeland.

(Bede – *De Templo*)

May the Saviour of the world, who stooped to assume the form of your humiliation, bless you, and by the intercession of the most holy Virgin Mary mercifully absolve you from the chains of your sins.

May he permit you to obtain the benefits of his grace by the merits of blessed Michael the Archangel and all the heavenly powers, whose feast day you devoutly celebrate today.

May the Lord protect you from the machinations of all who envy and hate you, by the guardianship of the apostles, under whose protection and discipline He has placed you.

May your Redeemer commend you to the assistance of his holy martyrs, and so liberate you from all opposition from your enemies.

May the Lord bless you by the prayers and merits of his holy confessors, who filled their hearts with the grace of the Holy Spirit.

May the Redeemer of humanity deign to bless you by the hidden merits of his holy virgins, whom he granted to triumph inviolately, both men and women.

As he has raised with his own right hand these holy virgins and all the saints, which the whole world celebrates today, to share in heaven and paradise, so may you by their hard-won merits and intercession be made worthy to possess the kingdom of heaven in all joy. Amen.   (*CB*)

Willibrord of Utrecht

7 November

Willibrord went to Frisia as a missionary from
the Northumbrian Church. He secured support from the
Frankish king and also from the Pope, Sergius,
who consecrated him bishop in 695. He created a diocesan
mission centre at Utrecht, and in 698 founded
a monastery at Echternach. He died in 739
aged eighty-one.

O Lord Jesus Christ, you call to yourself whom so ever you will
and send them whither you choose: we thank you for calling
your servant Willibrord to preach your gospel to the nations. We
humbly ask you to raise up among us faithful men and women
who will go forth to challenge the forces of evil and oppression,
and build up your Church in lands which do not know you, for
you live and reign with the Father and the Holy Spirit, one God
now and for ever. Amen.   (Traditional)

Care of all the churches

*Four days before Willibrord arrived in Rome, Pope Sergius had a
dream in which he was advised by an angel to receive him with
great honour, as he had been chosen by God to bring the light of the
Gospel to many people. His request to be made a bishop was to be
accepted.*

The Pope received him with great joy and honour, and quickly realised that he was a man of deep faith, devout prayer and genuine wisdom. He publicly consecrated him as Archbishop in the church of St Peter, calling him 'Clement', and robing him as a bishop complete with the pallium. He gave him whatever liturgical stuff he needed, and the relics of many saints. Then fortified with the Pope's blessing, Willibrord returned, laden with gifts, and duly commissioned to preach the gospel of Christ.

(Alcuin – *Life of Willibrord*)

Martin of Tours

11 November

Martin died in 397, and became one of the most influential of saints in the Frankish and English Churches. His *Life* by Sulpicius Severus became a model for later saints' lives, and his example as a monk-bishop and missionary became the measure for episcopal leadership and initiative towards secular rulers.

O God, you gave blessed Martin to be a minister of eternal salvation to your people. We pray that as we have him for our teacher of the spiritual life on earth, so we may be worthy always to have him as our intercessor in heaven. We ask this through Jesus Christ our Lord. Amen.

(*PW*)

In the world but not of it

It is unfair to compare Martin directly with the famous hermits of the desert. For they were free from all cares, living in the face of heaven, with only the angels as their witnesses. Thus they learnt how to achieve miracles.

But Martin by contrast lived as a bishop in the midst of crowds of people, fully engaged with their affairs, and harassed by quarrelsome clergymen and angry bishops. Scandals surged around him daily, but he stood fast with unshakeable virtue, in the face of all manner of distraction. There he performed miracles that surpassed in their way those wrought in the desert. (*Sulpicius Severus*)

Hilda of Whitby
19 November

Hilda was one of the most notable of the seventh-century English saints. She was baptised by Paulinus, and in the second part of her life became a nun, founding a small convent with the help of Aidan. She moved to Whitby in 657, and made it a centre of learning and Christian culture, of which the story of how the cowherd Caedmon learnt to compose poetry in English is just one glimpse. She died in 680.

Let us now praise the Creator of the heavenly realm,
The might of the Maker of all things and his wisdom,
The feats of the glorious Father, the eternal God,
The fountain of wonder, who first made the heavens as a roof,
Who designed the earth for the children of men,
He their Guardian all-powerful.

(Caedmon's song)

A mother to the Church

She devoted herself over many years to establishing the Rule of monastic life in her monastery at Whitby. She taught her community, both men and women, to observe the great virtues of justice, piety and chastity, ruling them in peace and love. True to the example of the earliest Church, none was rich, none in need, for they shared all things in common and there was no private property allowed.

Everyone came to her for advice, including kings and nobility. She compelled those in her care to allocate regular time for study of the Bible, and other time for good works, in order to train them up for the sacred ministry of the Church. All who knew Hilda called her 'Mother', for she was outstanding as a servant of Christ, and full of grace. (Bede – *History*)

Edmund the Martyr

20 November

Edmund was killed in 869 by marauding Vikings, having
refused to surrender his people to their rule. He died unarmed
calling upon Christ. Alfred the Great and his bishops promoted
the memory of the martyr-king to appeal to the loyalties of the
Christian English under Danish rule. The story of his death,
included among the Passiontide readings, was a living memory
as late as the time of Dunstan.

Almighty and eternal God, you kindle in the hearts of your
saints the fire of your love. Grant to us the same virtue of faith
and love, that as we rejoice in their triumphs, so we may be per-
fected after their example, in the following of your Son, our
Lord Jesus Christ. Amen.   (*PW*)

The chain of remembrance

*A certain learned monk came from the south, over the sea from St
Benedict's monastery at Fleury. This was during the reign of King
Ethelred. His name was Abbo, and he came to see Archbishop Dunstan
three years before he died.*

*They were in conversation and Dunstan told him about St Edmund,
even as he had heard Edmund's sword-bearer, then an old man, tell the
story to King Athelstan when Dunstan was a very young man. Abbo
later put the story into a Latin book, and when it reached us, we soon
turned it into English just as it stands here.*

*Abbo went home after two years in England to his own monastery,
and was shortly afterwards made its abbot. There he died a violent
death from a mob, a book in his hand.*   (Aelfric – *Homily on Edmund*)

.

PEREGRINATIO

A Pilgrim's Guide to Sites of
the Anglo-Saxon Church

Bewcastle, Cumbria	Carved standing cross from seventh century
Breedon, Leicestershire	Eighth-century carvings in church
Bosham, Sussex	Fine eleventh-century royal church
Baltonsborough, Somerset	Birth-place of St Dunstan
Barton-on-Humber	St Peter's church tower
Bradford-on-Avon, Wiltshire	Unique stone church of either seventh or tenth century
Bradwell-on-Sea, Essex	Cedd's church from the seventh century
Breamore, Hampshire	Eleventh-century church of St Mary
Brixworth, Northamptonshire	The most outstanding Anglo-Saxon church remaining
Canterbury	Pre-Saxon church of St Martin
	Ruins of St Augustine's abbey: burial-place of St Augustine and other early archbishops of Canterbury
	Cathedral: burial-place of St Dunstan and St Alphege
	Reculver cross shaft in crypt of cathedral
Cambridge	St Benet's church – eleventh century
Daglingworth, Gloucestershire	Carvings in parish church

Deerhurst, Gloucestershire	Outstanding Minster church with carvings
Durham	Burial-places of Cuthbert and Bede in cathedral
	Art works from Cuthbert's tomb in Treasury
Earls Barton, Northamptonshire	Fine church tower
Ely, Cambridgeshire	Outstanding late Anglo-Saxon carvings in Norman cathedral
Escomb, County Durham	Small private church from seventh century
Farne Islands	Site of Cuthbert's cell and chapel: a boat-ride from Seahouses
Fulda, Germany	Burial-place of St Boniface
Florence	Laurentian library: Codex Amiatinus of Bible from Jarrow
Glastonbury, Somerset	Site of abbey reformed by St Dunstan; good museum
Greenstead, Essex	Only wooden Anglo-Saxon church remaining
Hereford	Cathedral library: seventh-century Gospels
Hexham, Northumberland	Crypt built by St Wilfrid; his throne
Jarrow, Tyneside	East end of parish church dates from Bede's time
Lastingham, North Yorkshire	Crypt of present church contains some Anglo-Saxon remains from monastery there; Kirkdale church nearby has late Saxon sundial and inscription

Lichfield	Cathedral library: seventh century Gospels
Lindisfarne	Site of monastery and Cuthbert's first hermitage
London	St Dunstan's, Stepney – late Anglo-Saxon foundation
	British library – Lindisfarne Gospels and numerous Anglo-Saxon manuscripts
	British Museum and Victoria & Albert Museum – Anglo-Saxon artefacts and works of art
	Westminster Abbey: burial-place of St Edward the Confessor
Malmesbury, Wiltshire	Twelfth-century English carvings in Norman abbey church: burial-place of king Athelstan
Monkwearmouth	West front and porch date from Bede's time
North Elmham, Norfolk	Site and foundations of the tenth-century cathedral
Oxford	Ashmolean Museum: the Alfred jewel
	Binsey church: site of St Frideswide's cell
	St Michael-in-the-Northgate: tenth-century tower
	Iffley church: twelfth-century English carving
Reculver, Kent	Site and ruins of significant tenth-century monastic church within Roman fort

Repton, Derbyshire	Crypt contains Anglo-Saxon remains of monastery
Ripon	Crypt in cathedral built by St Wilfrid
Rome	San Gregorio al Celio: site of St Gregory's monastery from which St Augustine came; Gregory's cell and chair remain
	Santa Maria in Cosmedin: decorated eighth-century church, exemplar of style copied in England by Anglo-Saxons
	Quattro Coronati: early medieval monastery dating from time of St Gregory on Caelian hill
Romsey, Hampshire	Late Anglo-Saxon carvings of the crucifixion in the abbey church
Ruthwell, Dumfriesshire	Famous carved standing cross of eighth century
Selham, Sussex	Small late Anglo-Saxon parish church
Sheppey, Kent	Parish church built into corner of Roman watchtower
Stow-in-Lindsey, Lincolnshire	St Mary's eleventh-century church
Wells	Foundation outline of Minster church, and remains of late Anglo-Saxon bishops' graves
Whitby, North Yorkshire	Museum of excavation of St Hilda's monastery

Winchester	Outline of the Old Minster by the cathedral
	City museum
	Headbourne Worthy church
York	Crypt under Minster contains earliest site of church
	'Jorvik' exhibition of Viking life in the tenth century

FURTHER READING

The Latin prayer books

Birch, W. de Gray (ed.), *An ancient manuscript* (Nunnaminster Codex), *Hampshire Record Society*, 1892

Hughes, A. (ed.), *The Portiforium of St Wulfstan*, Henry Bradshaw Society, lxxxix, 1956/8

Woolley, R. M. (ed.), *The Canterbury Benedictional*, Henry Bradshaw Society, li, 1917 (reprinted by the Boydell Press, 1995)

Principal texts in translation

Alexander, M. (ed.), *The Earliest English Poems*, London, 1966

Boenig, R. (ed.) *Anglo-Saxon Spirituality; Selected Writings*, New York, Paulist Press, 2000

Campbell, A. (ed.), *Ethelwulf's 'De Abbatibus'*, Oxford, 1962

Colgrave, B. (ed.), *Two Lives of St Cuthbert*, Cambridge, 1985

Connolly, S (ed.), *Bede on the Temple*, Liverpool, 1995

Farmer, D. H. (ed.), *The Age of Bede*, London 1983

Hurst, D (ed.), *Forty Gospel Homilies: St Gregory the Great*, Cistercian Studies, Michigan, 1990

Lapidge, M.& Herren, M. (ed.), *Aldhelm's Prose Works*, Ipswich, 1979

McClure, J.& Collins, R. (ed.), *Bede's 'Ecclesiastical History'*, Oxford, 1994

Martin, L.T.& Hurst, D (ed.), *The Homilies of Bede* (2 vols.), Cistercian Studies, Michigan, 1991

Morris, R (ed.), *The Blickling Homilies*, Early English Text Society (repr) 1967

Skeat, W (ed.), *Aelfric's Lives of the Saints*, Early English Text Society (repr) 1960

Symons, T (ed.), *The Regularis Concordia*, London, 1953

Secondary Reading

Backhouse, J., Turner, D.H., & Webster, L.(ed.), *The Golden Age of Anglo-Saxon Art 966 - 1066*, London, 1984

Campbell, J. (ed.), *The Anglo-Saxons*, London, 1982

Dales, D.J., *Called to be Angels: an Introduction to Anglo-Saxon Spirituality*, Canterbury Press, 1998

Dales, D.J., *Dunstan: Saint and Statesman*, Cambridge, 1988

Dales, D.J., *Light to the Isles: Missionary Theology in Celtic and Anglo-Saxon Britain*, Cambridge, 1997

Farmer D.H., *The Oxford Dictionary of Saints*, Oxford, 1978

Levison, W., *England and the Continent in the Eighth Century*, Oxford, 1946

Mayr-Harting, H., *The Coming of Christianity to Anglo-Saxon England*, London, 1991

Ward, B., *High King of Heaven: Aspects of Early English Spirituality*, London, 1999

Ward, B., *The Venerable Bede*, London, 1990

Webster, L., & Backhouse, J.(ed.), *The Making of England: Anglo-Saxon Art & Culture 600–900*, London, 1991

ACKNOWLEDGEMENTS

page

14 The Lindisfarne Gospels, British Library BL Cotton MS Nero D iv (f.211)
    © Copyright The British Library.

18 The Missal of Robert of Jumièges, Rouen, Bibl. Municipale MS Y6 (f.32v)
    Collection de la Bibliothèque municipale de Rouen. Photographers Didier
    Tragin/Catherine Lancien.

25 The Franks Casket, London, British Museum (ivory: 23x13x19cm)
    © Copyright The British Museum.

28 The Lindisfarne Gospels, BL Cotton MS Nero D iv (f.137v) © Copyright The
    British Library.

32 The Lindisfarne Gospels, BL Cotton MS Nero D iv (f.139) © Copyright The
    British Library.

38 The Canterbury Psalter, BL MS Arundel 155 (f.93r) © Copyright The
    British Library.

42 The Tassilo Chalice, Kremsmünster, Austria (silver gilt: 27cm) Copyright Stift
    Kremsmünster (Upper Austria) art collections. Photographer Norbert
    Artner, Linz 2000.

49 The Brussels Cross, Cathedral of Saints Michel et Gudule, Brussels, (oak,
    silver and gilt: 559cm) Copyright IRPA-KIK, Brussels.

52 The Benedictional of Archbishop Robert, Rouen, Bibl. Municipale MS Y7
    (f.216) Collection de la Bibliothèque municipale de Rouen.
    Photographers Didier Tragin/Catherine Lancien.

58 The Codex Amiatinus, Florence, Bibl. Medicea Laurenziana MS Amiatinus 1
    Copyright Biblioteca Medicea Laurenziana, Florence/Microfoto srl.

62 The Benedictional of Archbishop Robert, Rouen, Bibl. Municipale MS Y7
    (f.29v) Collection de la Bibliothèque municipale de Rouen.
    Photographers Didier Tragin/Catherine Lancien.

68 The Benedictional of St Ethelwold, BL MD Add. 49598 (f.70r) © Copyright
    The British Library.

81 St Cuthbert's Pectoral Cross, Durham Cathedral (gold, garnets, glass, shell:
    6cm) Durham Cathedral.

90 St Dunstan's Classbook, Oxford, Bodleian Library MS Auct. F4 32 (f.1r)
    © Copyright The Bodleian Library, University of Oxford.

96 The Tiberius Bede, BL Cotton MS Tiberius c ii (f.5v) © Copyright
    The British Library.

103 Crucifix, London, Victoria & Albert Museum (ivory, gold & cedar: 18.5cm)
    © Copyright Victoria & Albert Museum.

Textual decoration:
The chapter head foliage scroll is from the border of Bede's *Lives of
    St Cuthbert*, King Aethelstan presents the Life of St Cuthbert to the saint.
    Corpus Christi MS 183. Copyright The Master and Fellows of Corpus
    Christi College, Cambridge.
The acanthus capital as text breaks is from The Arenberg Gospels M.869.
    (f.126v) Copyright The Pierpont Morgan Library/Art Resource.
The large and small roundels on part titles and chapter opening pages are
    from The Ramsay Benedictional MS lat. 987 (f.41). Copyright Cliché
    Bibliothèque nationale de France, Paris.